Urban Concepts
Denise Scott Brown

NIGHT VIEW, HENNEPIN AVENUE, MINNEAPOLIS

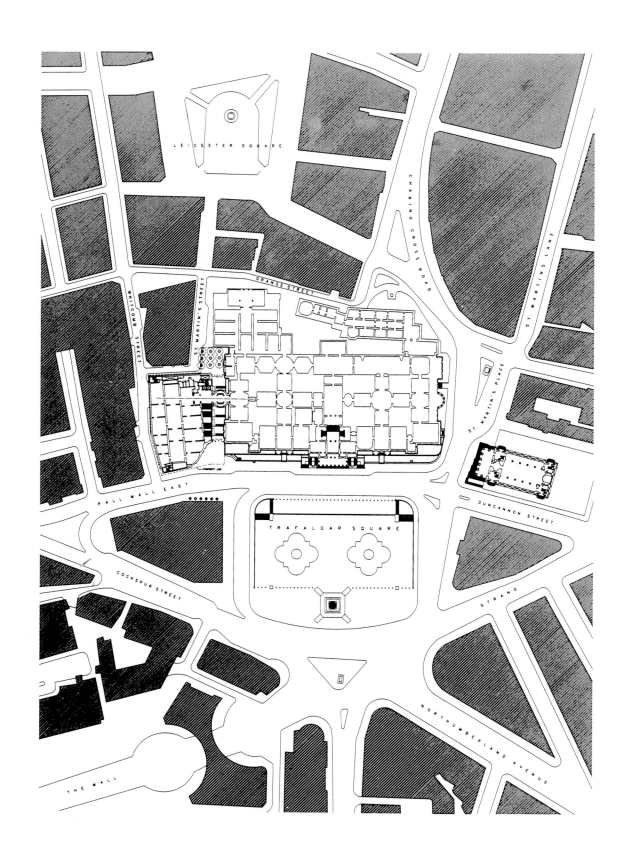

SITE PLAN OF NATIONAL GALLERY EXTENSION

An Architectural Design Profile

Urban Concepts
Denise Scott Brown

LAS VEGAS STRIP BY DAY

ACADEMY EDITIONS • LONDON / ST. MARTIN'S PRESS • NEW YORK

Denise Scott Brown
A Biographical Note

Since 1986, when they won the competition for the Sainsbury Wing of the National Gallery, the firm Venturi, Rauch and Scott Brown has been known in London. In this capacity and in the profession, these architects are not customarily identified with community architecture as it is understood in England. London architects were therefore puzzled to see notice of a lecture 'The Rise and Fall of Community Architecture' to be given by Denise Scott Brown at the Tate Gallery, in September 1988. 'What does she know about it?' they asked us. Those who heard the lecture saw an unexpected side of the firm, one that throws an interesting light on their architecture.

Denise Scott Brown's own role in her firm, as an inter-disciplinary, cross-continental link and a collaborator in translating urban ideas into architectural terms, is also not well known. In the following essays, which are in part autobiographical, she surveys the richness of architectural and urbanistic thinking that has emerged from the 'three disciplines and three countries' of her professional experience and suggests that urban ideas that are meaningful to Venturi and Scott Brown could be useful to others.

Denise Scott Brown was born in Zambia and raised in South Africa. In 1952, part–way through her architectural training she transferred to the Final School at the AA and continued in the Tropical School the first year it started. Subsequent work in the offices of Erno Goldfinger and Dennis Clarke Hall was followed by work and study travel in Europe and Africa. In 1958 she entered the University of Pennsylvania, in Philadelphia, where she received Masters Degrees in City Planning and Architecture. Apart from a few years in California, she has lived in Philadelphia since 1958. Scott Brown taught city planning, architecture and urban design for ten years at the Universities of Pennsylvania, Berkeley, UCLA and Yale. Scott Brown and Venturi have collaborated as colleagues since 1960 and were married in 1967. Since that time she has been a member of 'VRSB'.

Denise Scott Brown here describes the intellectual history of a set of ideas that were at the initiation of Post-Modernism and shows they are more wide ranging than is realised. She gives an account of her own work in the firm and discusses its relation to the work that she does in collaboration with Venturi. At the end, the transcript of a panel discussion after the Tate Gallery lecture reveals a fascinating confrontation between British and American ways of seeing urbanism, with Scott Brown performing what is perhaps her most useful function – linking things together.

For Robert Venturi

Editor: Dr Andreas C Papadakis

First published in Great Britain in 1990 by *Architectural Design*
an imprint of the
ACADEMY GROUP LTD, 7 HOLLAND STREET, LONDON W8 4NA
ISBN: 1-85670-955-7 (UK)

Architectural Design Profile 83 is published as part of *Architectural Design* Vol 60 1/2-1990
Published in the United States of America by
ST MARTIN'S PRESS, 175 FIFTH AVENUE, NEW YORK 10010
ISBN: 0-312-03067-3 (USA)

Printed and bound in Singapore

Contents

WASHINGTON AVENUE, MIAMI BEACH

Paralipomena in Urban Design 6
Between Three Stools 8
Public Realm, Public Sector and The Public Interest in Urban Design 21
Rise and Fall of Community Architecture 30

Urban Design Reports
Jim Thorpe, Pennsylvania 52
Princeton, New Jersey 58
Hennepin Avenue, Minneapolis 62
Washington Avenue, Miami Beach 70
Peabody Place and Beale Street, Memphis 76
Republic Square, Austin 88
Bibliography 96

PARALIPOMENA IN URBAN DESIGN

HULFISH STREET AT PALMER SQUARE, PRINCETON

When I taught planning and urban design, I found it fascinating to watch a good architect learn to be an urban designer. I first realised the extent of the change required when helping a young Central American architect with some years of professional experience cope with the demands of urbanism in a new city project. His dilemma was what to show in the blank spaces between streets in his

neighbourhood plan. He couldn't design every house. Even if he could in the studio, he knew that in 'real life' he would not. Was there some way to suggest houses without designing them? Should the suggestions show an intended architectural character? Should this be the one he hoped for or the one he thought would happen? What, beyond their architectural character, was important to the plan about these houses? Even were he to design the housing for the first families in the neighbourhood, how many others would follow, and how could he know their needs?

I saw these questions challenge this architect's design philosophy. As a result, he loosened up and produced, not a specific design that he liked, but a generic pattern, roughly as he expected it would evolve in the circumstances, given the directives of the plan and the level of guidance the planning agency in this developing area could reasonably be expected to exert. The experience was, I believe, salutory to him as an architect.

Architects in our planning school pored over plans and aerial photographs of cities, trying to understand how they got to be the way they were. Students learned to discern trends and to base their designs on an understanding of trends. They were, on occasion, edified to discover that what they intended to recommend had already come about in the city, proving they were on the right track.

Aspirant urban designers were faced with subjects they could not have dreamed would interest them - regional economics,

urban demographics, transportation analysis, or statistics - taught by teachers who were not architects nor concerned with the physical aspects of their subject. From this difficult stuff the students were required to elicit the determinants of urban form, and to interpret these determinants as designers. The course work was, as one student put it, like foul medicine: 'You take it and it tastes bad, but you get better.' I was there to see that the medicine improved their skills but did not inundate their creativity. Having trodden a similar path myself, and because I shared with many urban design students a European ancestry, a Third World origin, and a need to understand America, I was well placed to help them cope with the unfamiliar ideas of urbanism.

These ideas are largely excluded from architectural and urban design education, yet they have been important to me as an architect. Much of my professional life has been spent trying to connect urban thought with architecture. Although few architects or urban designers have had the training I describe above, some, especially in Europe, are fascinated by it. They ask how I learned to do the work I do and inquire about its relation to our architecture. I write primarily for these people. Urban concepts that Venturi and I have found particularly relevant to our theory and that inform the architecture of our firm, are the subject of this study.

'Paralipomena' means 'things that have been left out'. I stole my title from Paul Kriesis, who gave me a copy of his article,

'Paralipomena in Town Planning', in the mid-1950s. Kriesis railed against plans that were only beautiful pictures and were unsuited to people 'who were lacking not what planners thought necessary, but the very essentials for subsistence'. He was sceptical about the importance of aesthetics in planning, he admonished planners to distinguish between facts and values in their work; he denied scientists the right to judge values and called on planners to set out the value judgements upon which plans were based. He felt plans should be 'fully justified by actual political and economic conditions and deal to such an extent and for such a period as can be reasonably foreseen'. He argued that 'no ideal plans are required by *ideal possible* ones'. My paralipomena are largely his.

Although our architectural theory has been widely published and appraised, these aspects of its origins are not known. Post-Modern theory places the source of Post-Modernism in the Pop Art movement, the reappraisal of traditional architecture, and architects' and clients' boredom with the Modern Movement. There were two other important sources for us: the first, urban social concepts promulgated in the social sciences in the 1950s and applied in cities during and after the turbulence of the 1960s; the second, some ideas of the New Brutalists in England in the 1950s.

These other strains of thought in our work have been recognised by few architectural historians and critics, because most lack the cross-continental and interdisciplinary span to do so. Also, the high-profile critics are interested primarily in built work; they are not drawn toward social thought and they avoid difficult images; they are reluctant to read, and they prefer the work of gurus. Where social planning ideas have been explicitly discussed in our writing, as they were for example in *Learning from Las Vegas*, they have been ignored. We consider these ideas, nonetheless, vital to our architecture and believe that, to the extent they are omitted from the discussion of our work and thought, our architecture is misunderstood. We feel that, because we grapple with these difficult concepts, our work differs from that of the Post-Modernists. (Another major difference is that Robert Venturi's knowledge of history is both more profound and more broadly based than that of the Post-Modernists.)

Is what I am describing PoMo urbanism? No, but it's the urban theory from which our architecture derived. Our debate with Late-Modern architecture was initiated in considerable measure (though not of course exclusively) through social concern. Our 'Learning from Las Vegas' research project and our South Street community planning project were conducted at the same time. Therefore, we smart to hear our ideas on popular culture described as 'cynical populism', and to read that our architecture is lacking in social conscience. The techniques of deferring judgement that we recommended in *Learning from Las Vegas* were just that, techniques. Their aim was to make subsequent judgement more sensitive. Our buildings since then show what we did in fact learn from Las Vegas. A most important lesson was the need to understand and respond to an urban context that is broader than the physical.

While trying to help students make sense of urban information, I discovered that they could handle an unfamiliar and difficult subject more easily if I started with its history and showed how its ideas arose out of demands being made at the time. For this reason, in what follows I have frequently put forward my ideas by recounting my own experience. This profile covers a span of forty years but its essays were written in the decade of the 1980s. They were presented as papers to groups of architects and urban designers. Although I have edited and enlarged them to make their argument coherent, I have allowed differences in style, based on differences in subject matter and audience, to remain.

Because Robert Venturi and I have collaborated as academics and practitioners over the last 30 years, our ideas have grown together and there is no clear cleavage between our professional roles; we each are 'both/and', and we make a 'difficult whole' – too difficult for the critics, who have abandoned the task of accurate attribution. The pages that follow show the many others to whom I owe an intellectual debt of gratitude. It's been a joy to piece together their motley, setting the fragments where they fit in the fabric of my ideas and experience. The garb, and how I wear it, is my own.

LAS VEGAS

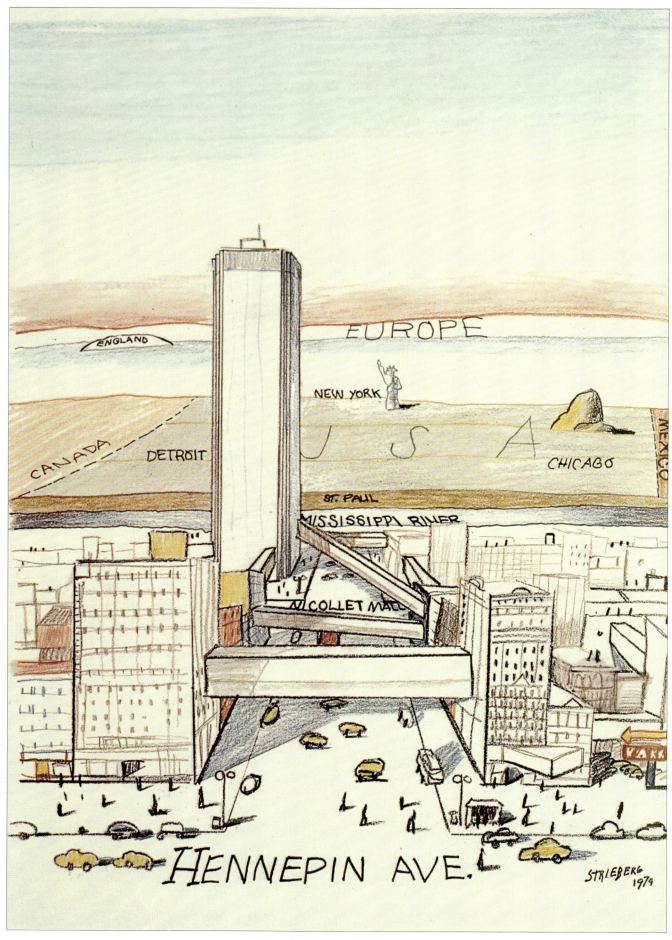

MINNEAPOLIS SELF IMAGE

BETWEEN THREE STOOLS
A Personal View of Urban Design Pedagogy

For a young architect studying at the Architectural Association in London during the early 1950s, the proper focus of architecture was urbanism. This had been true during the 1930s as well, when young architects, who were lucky enough to find clients for quite small houses, met at European CIAM Conferences to study the higher things of architecture, the philosophy of urbanism. During the War dreams were hatched, and after the War there were real prospects of realising these dreams in the rebuilding of European cities. Indeed, many architects saw their proper function and main opportunity as employment in governmental agencies conducting post-war rebuilding on a large scale. Through the AA passed a generation of high-minded, ex-service students whose vision melded social concern, CIAM rhetoric and a future for themselves in the housing division of the London County Council architectural office.

Teaching at the AA was Arthur Korn, a German refugee, late of the Bauhaus and a member of the English team that produced the MARS plan for post-war London. Korn's communist rhetoric, his Utopianism, his social view of architecture and his great-hearted pedagogic style imbued us with a mission. We were to be commandos for social change and regeneration through architecture – Korn's commandos.

So we 'Caught a whiff of the powder', as Peter Smithson once described it, of the much earlier architectural revolution of the 1910s and 1920s. But there were differences. Korn's own interpretation of how the physical form of the city resulted from the structure of the society was an important added ingredient. Also, by the early 1950s the New Brutalists were influencing the outer fringes of student thought at the AA.

Peter and Alison Smithson, and later their colleagues on Team 10, turned first to the exciting early stages of the Modern Movement, to International Style architecture in Europe. But at the same time they picked up where CIAM urbanism had left off and again the proper discourse for post-war CIAM Conferences became the rebuilding of cities. However, CIAM urbanism as defined by the Athens Charter, was less inspiring to them than was early Modern architecture. Quite soon a Brutalist critique of 1930s architectural urbanism appeared. The Brutalists favoured a much looser, less doctrinaire view of urbanism, one tied to local neighbourhood and community development. This 'active socioplastics', as Smithson called it, was not a direction in English architectural thought that survived beyond the 1950s. However, I found it irresistible.

For a neophyte European with an African background, this strange mixture of CIAM, Korn, post-war socialism and New Brutalism was a wonderful elixir. I think it formed the foundation for most of my subsequent thinking about architecture.

It wasn't only the social concern. Of equal importance to the Brutalists was Le Corbusier's complaint against 'eyes which do not see'. Starting with the grain elevators and liners that Le Corbusier used as examples of beauty unappreciated, the Brutalists opened their eyes to machines, folk architecture, even popular architecture and advertising and finally to uncomfortably direct architectural solutions that ignored the canons of architectural taste. 'Dualities' were good because studio critics said they were bad. 'Human Scale' as the architectural *summum bonum* was derided.

During these upheavals it was impossible that Mannerism should have gone unnoticed. In fact, John Summerson lectured at the AA on Classicism. I took his course twice. Through him, John Soane became a culture hero. Hawksmoor and Vanbrugh were respected antecedents. Edwin Lutyens received a friendly reappraisal (from Summerson; the Smithsons continued to give Lutyens a bad press). By now, some Brutalists were interested in uncomfortably *indirect* solutions as well as in uncomfortably direct ones. They had moved from eyes which do not see to facing the unfaceable, to enjoying the aesthetic shiver.

Real urbanism

Summerson helped open students' eyes. He also introduced us to real urbanism, not the CIAM kind. His lectures on Georgian London and Bath covered the tissue of buildings, squares and streets; described builders' housing that followed pattern books; and had us looking around us in London at the order in Georgian town architecture and the variety within the order. He showed us solutions others had found to archetypal problems in urban design such as the handling of corners of blocks and the marking of front doors.

Although Mannerist breaking of the rules was intriguing to Brutalists, it did not lead them to a profound questioning of the dogma of Modern architecture. Nor did Summerson's view of street architecture and the importance of continuity alter the students' need to re-make the world in the Modern image. At the AA if we were given a building to design between two others on a London street, most students would change the brief and re-plan the whole block. Those who stuck to the requirements and produced a town building were often called dentists, cavity fillers, by the faculty. When Arthur Korn began his lectures on city planning with a consideration of the economy of Western Europe a deputation of students asked him to step back and start with the economy of the world. My thesis, done with Brian Smith, was an urban project; workers' housing on a hillside site for a small Welsh mining village. It looked rather like a plan by Hilbersheimer (whose work I had not seen) and had a nascent megastructure rising part-way through it. However, owing to the influence of 'active socioplastics' each house was set resolutely on the ground. The next year, as students in the AA's Tropical School, we re-designed the city of Lima, Peru as a linear city; the mass transit was to travel at 300 kilometers per hour! And the next summer at the CIAM school in Venice, we did the same thing for the Venice region – obviously young architects from all over agreed that the proper focus for architecture was urbanism.

As a student at the AA, from my experience around studio, I had already begun to form the opinion that perhaps architects should not be town planners. They seemed to do too many things for aesthetic reasons and this was not justifiable when you considered the future of whole cities and regions. Who should be town planners then? I thought perhaps priests. They did things for moral reasons. Also at this time we met the Greek planner Paul Kriesis in London. One evening of conversation with him has remained with me all my life. He excoriated the view of planning that suggested it should be possible to move 120,000 people by fiat, and introduced us to pessimism, scepticism, pragmatism and conservatism as modes of thought suitable for urbanism. 'I'll be happy if I can say I have saved one street', he told us. A further reinforcing experience was work on a housing

9

project for Italian industrial workers in the office of Giuseppi Vaccaro, in Rome, in 1956.

Meanwhile, the Smithsons and Louis Kahn had met, with an implosion of ideas and a rippling of influences that has yet to be fully documented by architectural historians. For a while Lou Kahn was seen as a natural ally in socioplastics, a part of Team 10 in America. Putting all these experiences together it seemed obvious to us, when leaving the AA, that the best direction for committed architects, and particularly African ones, was toward 'town planning'. But town planning in England was a nuts-and-bolts affair, unrelated to CIAM urbanism. America was the place to study town planning and now there would even be a sympathetic home, in the unfriendly midst of capitalism, in the University of Pennsylvania where Lou Kahn was teaching. Peter Smithson recommended that the only place to apply to study town planning in America was the University of Pennsylvania.

We went home to South Africa, worked for architects and applied to the University of Pennsylvania, Department of City Planning. During that time a visit to housing areas outside Johannesburg introduced us in a realistic rather than Utopian and philosophic way to the terrors, wonders and complexities of

be the possibility of finding answers. At the end of one semester I could not believe that I had lived my life until then without the information I now had. Strangely, the exciting, radical urban visions of the students at the AA, *Ville Radieuse* and Miljutin's linear city, were sitting in staid textbooks and the most challenging ideas were coming from a group of social scientists who seemed sceptical of the architect's ability to help urban society in any way. Herbert Gans had recently moved to Levittown to be a participant-observer of the new society that was forming there. His course on urban sociology was one of the most scholarly I have taken. As much as Le Corbusier he cried against eyes which do not see, but the eyes were those of architects and urban planners and what they did not see was social reality. We argued volubly with him for one semester and became good friends. Urban economics, as it emerged from the discourse of five or six different economists, came to represent for me a method of understanding how the cost of effort could determine the form of the city, long before or regardless of the plans of urbanists. Economic theorists drew strange diagrams, intriguing for designers.

This was 1958 and 1959 and at Penn there were early stirrings

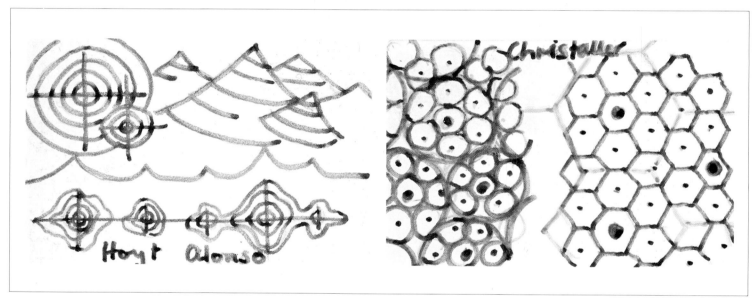

DIAGRAMS SHOWING ECONOMIST'S URBAN FORM, *L* TO *R*: HOYT ; CHRYSTALLER

mass housing and to many issues of development in 'developing areas', American ones too.

The University of Pennsylvania
Robert Scott Brown and I arrived at Penn in September, 1958. Our student adviser, David Crane, broke the news to us that Lou Kahn didn't teach in the planning school but added, 'Stay with us. There's much more to planning than you realise, coming from a European school. I'll help you make the most of your planning education and get the best out of Lou Kahn as well.' He scheduled no studio for us the first semester. We studied economics, urban sociology, housing, urban statistics and city planning history and practice with a group of faculty members and their assistants who were to become colleagues and friends for life – Wheaton, Mitchell, Rapkin, Gans, Davidoff, Harris, Isard, Reiner and many others. Their names should be much better known to American architects and urban designers than they are.

That first year we went spinning around like tops in the most interesting intellectual environment we had ever encountered. We had formulated a great many questions about architecture and urbanism while travelling and studying and here seemed to

of the social movements that were to rock the 60s. Social planning, which was to change the practice of planning and the curricula of planning schools over the next 15 years, was emerging at Penn. The architect in planning, the 'civic designer' was everyone's villain.

The social planners' critique of architects in urbanism was never very clearly formulated and its essence is hard to distil in a few paragraphs. Architects were first and foremost considered to be elitists and to be caught up in their own class biases. When I tried out on Herbert Gans Arthur Korn's assertion 'We are all workers', he replied snippily, 'Middle-class people don't like to talk about class. Most professional people have a value system and life style that places them within the upper-middle classes'. With that remonstrance in mind I have never denied being an elitist, but have tried to make myself aware of other people's values, particularly of those for whom I must plan or build. I have sought an understanding of the interplay of values that works itself out in urbanism and a comprehension of my leeway for action in a particular situation, depending on my role, the position of my client and my own moral values. I agree with Gans that planners should ask the politicians' questions – 'Who benefits? Who loses' – to keep them honest, at least with themselves.

Social planners accused architects and urban designers of bringing a 'physical bias' to urban planning, of trying to solve urban problems through planning streets and buildings, when often social or economic solutions would be more suitable. Architects, they felt, were well trained in coordinating and therefore became leaders of the planning team. However, owing to their ignorance, they tended to coordinate the wrong things. This meant that architects' team leadership in urban renewal had diverted that programme from a community support to a socially coercive boondoggle for developers.

Planning and urban design were not merely large-scale architecture and architects needed to enlarge their view of the urban world if they were to play the role they claimed in urban planning. The enlargement covered not only a much broader range of subject matter than most architects were prepared to stomach, from regional science to municipal government, but also an understanding of urban processes, their complexity, their time dimension and the multiple actors and decision-makers who brought them about.

On top of this, social planners felt that the architects' social-

It seemed to us that although most Americans' ancestors originated in Europe, they had had hundreds of years to diverge. Perhaps more important, many who left Europe were deviants in the first place and not only the Pilgrim Fathers. Six months of study in the social aspects of urban planning convinced us that the deviance was much greater than most Europeans realised. Americans, like many other nations, believed they had invented democracy but they seemed to mean something different and much more intense by it than the Europeans did. Also, six months in planning school convinced us that Americans had an inordinate tendency to document and analyse phenomena quantitatively. This we decided derived from the trauma of the Depression. But I discovered later that the same tendency had been noticed by De Tocqueville, more than 100 years earlier.

Penn planning studios
The next semester we entered studio, our heads full of scepticism and pragmatism. Dave Crane said 'You've been won over to the other side'. However, his studio, a re-planning of Chandigarh using Le Corbusier's programme but Penn's ideas, certainly

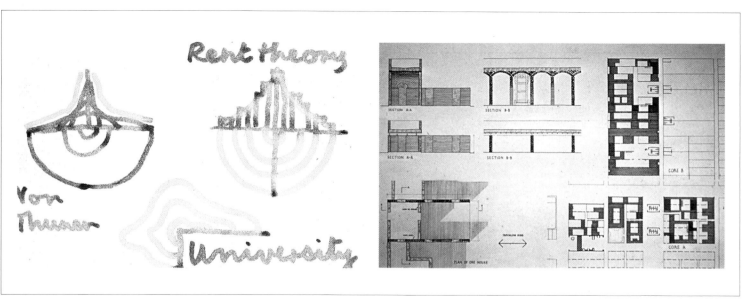

L TO *R*: ECONOMIST'S DIAGRAM OF URBAN FORM; SELF HELP HOUSING, NEW CITY, CHANDIGARH STUDIO, 1959

Utopian, CIAM visions and their simple-minded do-goodism, were more harm than help, particularly in urbanism for the poor. A better stance for the urban idealist was one of inspired scepticism, with a dash of pragmatism and a penchant for conserving, where possible, rather than destroying. The planners' critique was incoherent and much of it was incorrect – if architects were abolished we would still have urban problems. Its tone suggested that planning may indeed have found the priests I felt it needed. Its context is not new now, although many architects and urban designers have still to hear it. But to a pair of young idealists out of Africa and the AA it was some sort of killing lifeline. Although parts of it sounded like Team 10 and more like Paul Kriesis, it was basically different from anything we had learned as architects in Europe and Africa.

The 'Most Foreign Country'
The most striking perception of our first semester of American urban education was that 'city planning' in America was totally different from, much harder than, and very much more interesting than 'town planning' in Europe. We formed the opinion too that America was the most foreign country we had been in.

showed the influence of Penn's planning school. Planning studios at Penn were very different from architecture studios there or in any other school. The pedagogical theory was that in studio, the would be planner had the opportunity to coordinate the learning of course work and to focus it on practical problems, while at the same time developing skills which would be used in the field. In reality, the studios followed the ideas of the studio critics and were 'physically biased' but they were far more interdisciplinary than those in architecture schools. They were also much more structured. A preliminary research phase led to subsequent design phases. Students worked in small groups, first on research, then on alternative design concepts and finally on design development and implementation.

The attempt to interweave economics, law, demography, transportation, social studies and other areas of planning thought into the initial research of the studio but also into subsequent phases, and the need to help students develop a grasp on urban design and its theory at the same time, called for a hefty participation by the studio faculty in the project itself and in its planning – much more than would be required of an architectural studio critic. Crane's role was that of player-coach. For every studio he produced a small book of philosophy and work topics, one for each two students. Through his intense involvement, we too became close friends.

The pedagogical aim of a New City studio in a developing area, of which the Chandigarh studio was an example, was to remove the students from the complexity and detail of their own culture and surroundings, to intrigue them with information about a strange culture and to allow them to span, in one semester, a wide range of problems that might be difficult to handle close up. In planning for a developing area further issues arose that were related to the ideals we had brought with us. These concerned the rural poor who were urbanising at the outskirts of cities in developing areas and the need to find means of housing them that related to the scale and magnitude of the problem and not to some architect's concept of the ideal house. The possibilities of self-help; the idea of providing urban infrastructure rather than housing; the complex economics of urban development, where different types of capital were available for different types of jobs, fascinated us and dominated the studio. We virtually disregarded the part of the project that Le Corbusier had made his own, that is, the creation of a new set of urban symbols for India.

I was responsible for the housing section of this studio – the woman in the class usually was. It was one of my most exciting studio experiences. Our plans for Chandigarh caused great controversy at Penn, particularly in the architecture school. Lou Kahn sat shaking his head at what the social planners had wrought. His critique of the social planners was that they planned for statistical entities such as '2.5 people'. 'Sure cities are for people', he growled 'but you suspect that the person who tells you this learned it only yesterday'.

A poignant confrontation took place one day in a faculty meeting, sadly far from the students. It was between Kahn and Anthony Tomazinis, a transportation engineer and planner on the faculty at Penn. The issue was roughly between artistry and scientific rigour. Each was diehard in his view and their dedication to their professions was equivalent. Lou saw their differences most perceptively; 'We have reverence for different things. He for books, I for architecture'. Each resented interference from others in what he was most personally invested in. 'You can't do design by committee', stormed Lou. 'You can't do research by committee', thundered Tony.

At the final presentation of the Chandigarh studio was a young instructor named Robert Venturi. I didn't meet him until over a year later, when I was on the faculty at Penn.

In the summer of 1959, Robert Scott Brown was killed. I returned to school in the fall because no alternative seemed better. I took one studio with Lou Kahn in my final semester. I had met and talked with him several times after the Chandigarh presentation, partly because my Team 10 connections had made me want to ask him questions that few other students were considering at Penn in 1959. I also on occasion found myself arguing with him at juries. This was typical for English students but unusual for Americans and particularly so as the jury was not of my project or even my class. On one occasion I had a long argument with him on the design of a neighbourhood unit. The neighbourhood unit concept, I declared, was old-fashioned and out of date, restrictive socially and soft-headed in its desire to separate the pedestrian and the automobile. Another quite elderly member of the jury at this point added 'Well, indeed, we had intended to separate the pedestrian and the automobile at Radburn'. I gathered that this was Clarence Stein.

In CIAM fashion, Lou ran an urban studio. He and I fought all the way. I accused him of making irresponsible design decisions that gave architects a bad reputation with planners – for example, to close Walnut, Chestnut and Market Streets as they crossed Independence Mall in Philadelphia. The result was that we widened and dignified these streets as they passed through the Mall and created parking lots! Beautiful and ceremonial ones, to be sure. I think Lou enjoyed it and so did I, but again the architects on the faculty were horrified.

A Penn Professor

Toward the end of my final semester at Penn, I looked around and saw a course without an instructor. It was an introduction to urban design for non-architects. I asked David Crane if I could teach it. That was how I started teaching at Penn. I taught this course in the fall semester and was assistant to Crane for the New City studio in the spring. This focused my position in education and indeed in my professional life ever after. I operate at the nexus between architecture and planning. This may involve me in urban design, but there are other ways of relating architecture and planning, particularly as planning has shifted its focus toward the social sciences.

For the sceptical young social scientists, immersed in problems of poverty and Davidoff's Theory of Planning and stuck with having to take 'Denise's course in architecture', the pedagogical question was: Should they be required to 'know about' or to 'know' urban design? This was the difference between learning and learning by doing. Studio education, to me, involves learning by doing, so I tried to give them actual experiences in designing. Some were talented designers, and some, despite their hostility, were drawn into problems that they disdained intellectually but creatively could not put down. I had grumbling geographers staying up all night on problems such as 'Construct a model of an urban space whose coloured walls, if you were between them, would give you nightmares'. Or, 'Locate a six-foot, white marble cube somewhere on the campus and justify your choice of location.'

One project I devised for non-architect planners was called 'The Shipwrecked Planner'. It was based on the AA's introductory programme for first-year architects 'The Shipwrecked Architect' and its aim was similar; that is, to introduce many and complex design issues to incoming students before they had mastered manual and graphic skills. Posing as the leader of a group of planners who had set sail for a conference in a country named Developingarea, in flowery prose I described their plight, stranded on an island with one of four alternative types of climate and vegetation, beset by the need to protect themselves immediately and convinced that help would not come for at least six months. The necessity to keep together, the almost religious significance that look-out would play for the community and the fact that these were educated urbanites, not primitive people, were to direct the planning effort. The requirements were to produce a model, no drawings, and to build only what could be built with the surrounding resources and salvage from the wreck. Lou Kahn came to the jury and liked the religious look-out posts. I later saw this exercise published as an architectural game entitled 'The Stranded Planner'.

Another, perhaps prophetic, project was the design of an African market. This, too, was an AA programme (from the Tropical School) altered for non-architects. They were given a standard, modular market shelter. Their task was to group shelters into sequences of spaces suitable to their selling function. An important design constraint was that the local population could not read. The students were required to use signs, high picture signs, visible from the main entrance and other spots within the market, to direct customers to shopping enclaves where different goods could be bought. In the nature of an African market, only three transportation modes, service trucks, bicycles and pedestrians, were considered and low-cost sun protection was an important requirement.

In the spring I worked on the New City studio, first as an

assistant to the planning studio critic, eventually on my own. Using Crane's model, my studios had an early research phase followed by a brief sketch design. This in turn was succeeded by a more detailed research phase related to three or four alternative designs, which were selected from the sketch designs of the phase before. Students, collaborating in small groups, applied the research to elements of the plans, using it to develop more detailed designs. The final presentation contained a written report and drawings. The final jury was a grand interdisciplinary affair, where members of the faculty, whom the students met for coursework elsewhere in the planning programme, argued loudly with each other. The inspired fights between their faculty members were highly instructive to the students and, more than architectural juries, they felt entitled to take part.

Hamming and other aspects of studio pedagogy

Most important in engineering these grand battles was Professor William Wheaton, who first instructed me in the art of hamming in education. Scanning the problem and the jury members present, he would assume the role of some professional or lay person who was missing from the discourse. He could play the outraged ecologist, the scanted resident, the unserved industrialist or the scholarly academic, comparing the situation in Venezuela in 1960 with that in New York in 1840 or Russia in 1920.

This element of play has always seemed to me to be vital to studio. My last New City studio stressed regional economic development and industrialisation. Our problem was the communities of industrialised peasants that were forming the new city of Guayana in Venezuela. As important to us as their physical requirements was the social organisation of such communities for self-help and economic development. One student assigned herself the role of an imaginary Peace Corps worker in one community. Her project was a day-by-day diary, in letters home to her mother, describing the evolution of the community, socially, economically and physically.

The planning studio was subdivided to give each critic about 12 students. This group consisted of students in the joint regional science-planning programme, the planning department and the civic design programme. Some architects dealt with subjects such as demography and some social scientists emerged smudged with pastels from an encounter with 'physical planning'. I planned the intensity points in the studio, the charrettes, even before the subject subdivisions. The students' immersion as a group in the intense demand of studio, in the mutual adversity of the deadlines and in a problem that was fascinating and appealing to their social morality, engendered in the class a camaraderie that I felt was as educational as the subject matter. The students were proud of their work and demanded judgement from the jury, not merely comment. They got it, some of it rather harsh; I sat by proudly not saying a word as my students defended themselves on all scores.

It was necessary, I found, to prepare students carefully for such juries. They needed to know what the jury could and could not do in the time available. Having students question the jury, we discovered, helped to keep jury members constructive and respectful even when they were critical. Some of the most feared criticism, for the urban design students at least, was that their analysis and design were separate and unconnected; that the analysis was some kind of ritual dance for architects who were incapable of carrying through its findings, or even its quantities, into design. Some of the most interesting questions that came up at juries concerned the extent to which a design was an illustration, a prediction or a statement of intention. Through discussions of this sort, led in particular by Professor Robert Mitchell, architect planners learned to differentiate their role as urban designers from that as architects to individual clients.

After most juries, I conducted post-mortems with the students, to bind up wounds as well as to find out what we had learned from the jury process. I think my students were emboldened to take part actively in jury discussions and to reveal their own worries about their projects because they knew that I and not the jury was going to grade them.

With changes in the curriculum at Penn, the New City studio was abandoned and I moved to teaching the introductory studio for civic design students taking the join MArch-MCP degree. This programme, for 'particularly talented designers', filled the required courses for one degree into the electives of the other. The students received the bones of each programme but not much of the flesh of either. For quite a few, their first brush with the social sciences, transportation engineering and law was traumatic, not the least because they were unaccustomed to so much reading. In addition, the hostility of faculty members from these areas to architects placed an added burden on students who were not yet firmly established in their own field. I decided my introductory course should help civic design students get an overview of the interdisciplinary subject matter that they would address in more detail in following semesters. Also they needed to learn that there was an urban designer's way of approaching each subject, a way which was valid although different from the view of the lecturer and which was related to their original interest in architecture. 'But what does this (demography, succession-invasion, regression analysis) mean for an urban designer'? became my refrain, a refrain parodied, needless to say, in the student Christmas skits.

Form, forces and function

To handle this problem conceptually, I evolved the FFF studios ('Watch your language, Denise', said Paul Davidoff). Form, forces and function; the thesis was that the physical form of the city depends as much upon the forces within the environment, the society and its technology as it does on 'functions' as architects define them. Urban designers who study urban sociology in planning school, I argued, will get little help there in understanding how social arrangements influence physical form and even less help in relating sociological information to the task of designing cities. Urban designers will have to do the difficult job of bridging for themselves and my role is to help them do it. The students began with an intense period of reading. Then *they* became the teachers. Each student made him or herself responsible for reading in a chosen discipline from a selected bibliography and then for presenting the material to the class, from the standpoint of an urban designer. Thereafter we selected one or several design problems and, using our new information, tried to relate forces to form in a specific context. One context was Fortieth Street in West Philadelphia, which passes, along its length, through a series of different communities, like string through beads.

We discovered through these studios that urban designers must learn to define not only the forces but also the forms, because architectural form, as defined by Modern architects, throws little light on urban form. This led to a consideration of the definitions of Kevin Lynch, Fumihiko Maki and David Crane, among others. None were as useful as we hoped they would be. Also, we experimented with graphic methods of suggesting architectural and urban character without actually designing buildings, and with methods of depicting differences between design intentions and projections, between recommended actions and expected reactions and between graphic statements of fact and graphic statements of value.

Shortly after I joined the faculty at Penn in 1960, a series of all-day curriculum discussions was held by the planning department. The greats of the school were still all there and, as much as anything, these discussions formed the basis for my pedagogy and particularly for my theories of studio education. I learned a great deal about planning a studio from Britton Harris, a planner with economics background, who I don't think believed studio should be taught at all. I came to see studio not as a simulation of reality, but as a careful abstraction of aspects of reality to suit some pedagogical purpose. Not all aspects of reality can be simulated at once and no single studio should try; nor should all studios deal with the same portions of reality; in fact a mixture should be available during the length of a student's career. Some studios may stress analysis and research, others design. Some may tackle a 'root' problem, others a 'branch' problem. Being a cavity filler in some studios is a good idea. Being a world economist in others is also a good idea. But you probably shouldn't try to be both at one time. The art in studio planning lies in defining what is possible within the 15 or so weeks available and not jumping beyond those bounds. Also, and here I added my own ideas, 'design' should not apply to the physical city only and 'analysis' should not be considered a non-architectural activity only. There can be design for the economy and there can certainly be architectural analysis.

Studio under fire

Over the next few years a consensus developed among the planning faculty to abolish studio. By 1963, the social revolution had profoundly changed planning education at Penn. Paul Davidoff, a lawyer and planner and then and for all his subsequent career, an ardent warrior for the poor, became a campaigner for a new method and philosophy of planning. He developed his ideas, together with his colleague Thomas Reiner, through a course in the Theory of Planning, which had a strong following among the students and which in the form of an article, written with Reiner, was seminal in the social planning movement. The planning method they espoused was evolved to ensure the democratic participation of those planned for, as well as to promote rationality in the process of arriving at decisions. In outline, this method consisted of the listing of goals, the surveying of alternative means of achieving these goals, the democratic choice of one of these means and its development into a plan. This dictum had a terrible simplicity. It was criticised by the only students who had tried any form of planning method, the architects in civic design; and by me. I sat and kibbitzed through the whole course, pointing to the need for iterations and asides, side loops and caveats. But, although it underrates both artistry and analysis, it is really the only moral method of planning and I have tried to follow it as a practitioner.

Paul's pedagogy was based on his law school training. He used the Socratic method, squeezing the answer out of the student, then strongly questioning the student on the answer: 'Planning is a process? What d'you mean planning is a process? Planning isn't a process?' I enjoyed the Socratic method and found the interchanges invigorating, but it seemed to be more useful in debating the nitty-gritty issues of legal cases and in reviewing of existing knowledge than in breaking new ground. It was too verbal for many urban designers and, in Socratic discourse, new ideas were often attacked before they could be properly formed.

Paul attempted to advance his planning theory in a studio that he ran, called GAP. I can't remember what the acronym stood for but it was chosen advisedly to suggest a gap in planning education. The subject matter of the studio was the goals of the Philadelphia police force. It had no physical design in it at all. At the final jury, the head of the Philadelphia police force discussed with us the psychological insecurities of police officers. The goals of this particular studio were never altogether clear to me

but I think the students enjoyed it. However, those who criticised studio for its 'imperialism' – its ability to build empires in the school and monopolise the time of students – were not satisfied with such adaptations. 'Workshops' were substituted for studio. These had no creative, problem-solving tasks, from my viewpoint, the students in them did sums. I think the students agreed and found them boring 'busy-work'. (Actually, this is not fair comment. There is no item of pedagogy that I have not found some student somewhere to define as busy-work.)

At this time when studio was heavily under fire, a collaborative studio was conducted in the school of Fine Arts at Penn. It involved first year architecture, planning and landscape students. I thought it was a calamity. These beginning students were insecure in their own fields and therefore unable to countenance the rivalry between fields that went on in the studio. I saw neophyte social planners form strength-giving and sustained hostility to architecture in this studio. Their feelings were exacerbated by the fact that the architects in planning school were usually more mature than the non-architects (it was even indicative that we couldn't find a more positive name for them) because the architects had already gained one professional degree before coming to planning school. I don't believe in collaborative studios between entering students in rival professions. The collaboration should wait till they are more firmly grounded in their fields.

Paul Davidoff and I were friendly rivals as assistant professors. We had offices opposite each other in the basement of the Fine Arts Building and could lean over and argue without leaving our chairs. Arguments erupted too at the coffee machine. Students caught in the cross fire were amused and delighted. I think they were edified too. We set up a strong polarity in the context of a great deal of sympathy.

But I was in the rear guard of the battle for studio and went down fighting as it was abolished from the planning curriculum. Since then, it has been poignant and ironic for me to hear Paul Davidoff agree that studio is a wonderful form of pedagogy for professionals, based on his subsequent experiences as a professor elsewhere. In the early 1980s, schools of planning headed back toward the training of generalists, stress on a professional rather than an academic curriculum and even the reinstitution of something remarkably like studio. The pendulum swung, but not before our firm suffered considerably, as architects and urban designers, at the hands of planners who learned nothing in their training or subsequently about architecture or urban design, but who nevertheless made decisions about them.

Satellite courses and seminar

At the same time that I was teaching Penn planners about architecture and urban design, I was teaching Penn architects about planning and urban design. For first year graduate architecture students I ran a course entitled Theories of Architecture, Landscape Architecture and Planning. It was a three-ringed circus in which faculty members in the three fields expounded their philosophies for the students

The pedagogical theory that backed this course and dictated its position in the curriculum was Dean Holmes Perkins'. He conceived a cluster of courses, of which this was one, encircling and supporting the studio. Incoming students in a graduate programme, he argued, had well-developed verbal skills and good general knowledge but lacked manual and graphic ability and confidence. They should not be given an individual building to design, but rather a neighbourhood in the city. The first few weeks spent inventorying and documenting the neighbourhood could employ the students' verbal skills while it accustomed them to graphics and the use of architectural techniques. Later they could move from site planning to the design of individual units. Hence the theories course concentrated first on urbanism, to help students gain background and knowledge for their design task. But how do you help beginning architects, or even experienced architects to translate intellectual and verbal information into design? This question, which formed the nub of my teaching for the civic designers, was handled by Holmes Perkins, for architects, through the insertion, between the lecture course and the studio, of a seminar run by a young architect. This seminar helped students interpret the lecture material and relate it to their design problems, through examining, documenting and analysing existing buildings and complexes.

My task was to organise the lectures of the course and to run the seminar. I evolved work topics related to both the lectures and the studio problem, directed students to relevant examples, historical and modern, and criticised their efforts to draw them. The efficacy of this tutorial insertion was demonstrated by the drop in studio performance when it was abandoned.

Venturi at Penn.

During the spring semester, the theories course became more specifically architectural and was run by Robert Venturi. We had met in 1960 at Fine Arts School faculty meetings and had become friends when we discovered ourselves to be on the same side of many issues that divided the faculty; for example, one such question was, should the Furness Library at the University be saved or demolished? (It is unthinkable now that some people wanted to demolish it.) Bob was the only faculty member in the department of architecture at Penn, not excluding Kahn, whom I found to be in any way sympathetic with the ideas that I brought with me from England and with the concerns that were upheaving the planning school. He shared my AA friends' desire to face the unfaceable in architecture and, as they did, connected that way of thought with Mannerism. He liked the same things they did, dualities, juxtapositions of scales including violent juxtapositions and juxtapositions of symbols.

I started visiting Bob's office to give 'crits' and, when his teaching assistant left, suggested that he let me collaborate with him on his course by giving the tutorials. Bob's lectures were as profound, scholarly and well-prepared as Herbert Gans' had been. He listed the elements that define architecture today. This list included the Vitruvian elements but was expanded to deal with 20th-century exigencies such as mechanical equipment. Each element had a lecture devoted to it and, for each, a review of history was made, to derive theoretical positions. That was the scholarly part. How did Gothic architects deal with the problem of letting light into buildings and how did this compare with the views of Renaissance architects and of Louis Kahn on the same problem? At the end of each lecture Robert Venturi said what he felt on the subject. Those last parts he later developed further to form the book *Complexity and Contradiction in Architecture*. It provided the profound critique of Modern dogma and the new direction for architecture that, although they were incipient in the thought of Brutalists in the 50s and Penn social planners in the early 60s, were attained by neither group, nor by any other, before him.

For urban design, another aspect of Bob's teaching was equally important. Although the course was scholarly in its span and in its analysis, it was more professional than academic in its approach. Elements of history were viewed non-chronologically and comparatively and related to modern practice and problems, so that young architects could learn from them lessons suitable for their practice for today. This 'professionalising' of academic knowledge is, for me, the essence of professional pedagogy. It was what lay behind my eternal question to the urban design students 'What does this mean for urban design?' It holds the key to giving action-oriented professionals adequate knowledge

without paralysing them. I have always regretted that Bob didn't write a book on the first, and largest, part of each lecture as well. It would have been a professional's history and theory of architecture.

However, in the architecture school, Robert Venturi, to his disgust, was valued as a scholar rather than as a practitioner. He was not considered an 'urban designer' at Penn, because he dealt mainly with individual buildings. I found this outlook ridiculous and still do. Whether a building or building complex is 'urban design' or not, seems to me to lie, not in its size or its connectedness to other buildings, but in the way its design is approached. A suburban house can be a piece of urban design, even a teaspoon can be urbane and a downtown, multi-storey development can look as if it were designed to rise from a green field.

A change of hats

During my last year at Penn, I spent the fall semester teaching in the furore of the planning school, battling it out with Davidoff and the students on questions of democracy and equity, and the spring semester more contemplatively surrounded by slides, directing students designing a townhouse to the minor architecture of Venice and relating Bob's lecture on circulation to their problems in designing a school. This involved a definite change of hats. With each semester I became a slightly different person. This is probably endemic to the urban designer's role and part of the cause of the uncertain identity of the field. You do have to change when you shift between architecture and planning. The aim should be not to change too much. As it was, I diluted this shift by auditing a variety of courses every semester, in different subjects from sociology to computer sciences. I worked and argued with a range of colleagues as well: Robert Venturi, Herbert Gans, Walter Isard, Russell Ackoff, Britton Harris, Malcolm Campbell and, though not at Penn, Allard Lowenstein.

As a student, I did not take Penn's Civic Design option and believe I benefited thereby. I missed a few rather dull courses that were given specifically for civic design students but had the time to go beyond their purview into regional economics on the one side and theory of architecture on the other. The fact that my span has been so broad is probably more related to my own personal outlook than to the needs of all urban designers. Not everyone requires the breadth that I have described in order to design in an urban way and many prefer a more hands-on approach to architecture than I have had in the last 20 years.

The civic design students, too, had a hard time changing hats. Unfortunately, few planners showed any interest in architecture. The interdisciplinary faculty was required by the Dean to serve on juries in all school departments, but even so it was extremely difficult to get the planning faculty onto architectural juries; they thought it a waste of time. By the same token I had great difficulty getting architects into my civic design students' crits. I ensured that my students got crits from Bob Venturi, but in an extra-curricular way.

The real Philadelphia School

What I have described here is not the Philadelphia School that most architects know and that has been written about by architectural journalists or graduates from Penn's architecture department. But it is a better school than that and my description is more accurate than theirs for the broader School of Fine Arts.

The real importance of the real Philadelphia School for architecture and urbanism has yet to be defined. Few architectural historians or critics can assess so broad a programme. The social planners (whose influence is in abeyance even in planning schools, but who will surely reassert an important role in the profession with the next swing of the pendulum) have the breadth, but are blocked by their prejudices against architecture. The great years at Penn's School of Fine Arts didn't last long. In 1958, students went to Kahn's master class because they didn't get into Harvard. By 1965, many of the most interesting faculty members from Penn's architecture and planning departments had their own departments, or schools, or were honoured professors elsewhere.

In planning education at Penn, West Coast cities, particularly Los Angeles, were objects of interest rather than scorn. As young architects were expected to see Europe for the completion of their education, so young planners were not considered fully prepared until they had experienced West Coast urbanism. Therefore, when I was invited to visit the University of California at Berkeley for a semester, I accepted with alacrity, especially as I had not been re-appointed after my fourth year at Penn.

Getting Berkeley activists to read
I reached Berkeley in 1965 at the tail end of the Free Speech Movement and during the Foul Speech Movement. I taught an introduction to city planning to fourth year undergraduate architects and a seminar in urban form to graduate students in the planning department.

I found to my surprise that these uproarious architecture students, filled with moral indignation and outrage at conditions within their society, knew virtually nothing about these conditions professionally. They had no idea of the debate on the social value of architecture that rocked Penn and, when I discussed their profession's role in helping or hindering the conditions of the urban poor through urban renewal, I could tell from the shocked silence that no one had told them this before.

Also, they didn't want to read. Getting architecture and urban design students to read has been a major interest of mine. I find that they don't want to read architecture, let alone boring material in related fields that will make them better architects. I have tried various methods and ruses. The most successful is to chose a problem that is of great interest to the students. In the 1960s this meant it had to be an agin-the-government, iconoclastic problem. Then one must set the problem up in such a way that the students will have to do the assigned reading to find the answers they need to do their designs. This is the most surefire way to induce reading and the best for the students, as they will learn to do professional reading for a purpose that is close to their hearts. Learning in books will be seen as a useful resource. It will become less frightening.

The success of this method has led me to consider whether the separation between undergraduate and graduate education in architecture is altogether desirable. For example, undergraduate pre-architects who study sociology before they study architecture tend to define it as 'Sosh' and to forget it long before they deal with housing in studio. Whereas graduate students, who have the chance to take an urban sociology course while they are thinking hard about a problem in mass housing, will probably find the material useful and incorporate it into their professional identities. By the same token, Basic Design as a course should probably be taken by 18-year-olds, or perhaps by high school students. (The academic counter-argument, that professional courses should not sully the liberal arts years, appears to me to be misplaced. If the professional courses are nuts-and-bolts affairs that lack philosophy, they belong with voc ed, not the university.)

A second way to make architects read is to point out that they will have very little chance in their subsequent careers to think about their own philosophies and to read in order to help themselves find one. A reading list, to which is appended a requirement to try to formulate a personal philosophy in writing

and to which I have added: 'I really want to know what you think about these subjects, just tell me what you think. I won't grade you', is an attractive invitation to many graduate students.

At Berkeley, I used the FFF format to introduce the subject matter of city planning to young architects and found it was meaningful to them. To help them sum up their experience, I gave a 'let's pretend' paper, a simulation of something that they might face in their professional lives. They had received a letter of inquiry from a potential client regarding the development of a new city in the desert outside Phoenix, Arizona. They were to write a planning proposal, describing all the steps that would be involved in planning for this new town. They were to tackle the problem in small groups, preferably choosing collaborators whose opinions differed from theirs and arguing through the issues of urban development.

Action-oriented courses
The action-oriented term paper made the course rather like a studio. This seems suitable for students in professional schools. It is arguably also suitable for undergraduate students who are not headed for academic careers and particularly for social activists. I have often wondered whether more action-oriented coursework for Berkeley undergrads might not have helped them to get through their Free Speech Movement more comfortably.

Professional courses should, I believe, have juries, like studio. Here, faculty members from various subject areas and studio critics could argue the subject matter of the courses, from different viewpoints. I have always regretted that no students were present during the faculty meeting when Crane told Davidoff that every housewife knows she needs no more planning to run her household than is obsolutely necessary and no planning theory at all.

For the graduate seminar, I again used the FFF format and asked the students to analyse sections of San Francisco, showing how their form was determined by factors within the environment and the society. Unlike the undergraduates, these students were particularly mature and well-educated. Both architects and non-architects could grasp the material and use it to help synthesise what they had learned in planning school. We all enjoyed the opportunity to learn more about a beautiful city. I chose the subject of San Francisco advisedly, remembering how, as a student at Penn, I was too busy to get to know Philadelphia until the end of the first year.

I joined urban design curriculum discussions at Berkeley. The faculty was trying to decide whether to place urban design with planning or with architecture and had decided on two programmes, one in each department. The non-architectural Systems option within the planning department was, to me, by far the most interesting part of Berkeley's School of Environmental Design. The arguments of Mel Webber were as stimulating as those of the social planners at Penn and were, I felt, just as wrong-headed. At Berkeley, I came across Charles Moore's writings on California and found these interesting and relevant. Moore had obviously been more receptive to Webber at Berkeley than architects had been to planners at Penn. J B Jackson, who like me was visiting Berkeley that semester, became a good friend. His social vision of the urban, rural and agricultural landscape coincided in many ways with my social view of the physical form of the city. I admired the urbane scholarship he brought to his analysis of rural strips, for example, and was grateful to him for his recommendation of a book that helped me understand the determinants of urban form. It was *The Human Use of the Earth* by Philip Wagner. Later, when Bob and I had already published two articles on Las Vegas and were preparing for the Las Vegas studio at Yale, I read back issues of Jackson's *Landscape* magazine and realised that he had written in the same vein, rather better than we had and 10 years before us.

New school at UCLA

From Berkeley, I was hired by UCLA to help start a new school of architecture and urban planning. I was to be joint head (with Henry Liu) of urban design, the first programme to be offered at the school. The reasoning behind the decision to start with urban design was interesting and throws light on the urban design profession. UCLA was a big and complex university, with strength in the social sciences and in real estate. Through its traffic safety programme, it even had transportation engineers. There were programmes in art, art history, architectural history, and industrial design. There were, however, no planners or architects. To have set up professional programmes in architecture and planning would have required a large staff. However, to institute an urban design programme called for a few architects, including at least one with planning training and the use of the existing skills in other departments within the university. Such a programme could be arranged with minimal reorganisation and investment and could lead later to a larger school of architecture and planning.

We decided on an interdisciplinary format where studio was the main focus for all studies and took almost all of the students' semester credits. I was the first studio critic. I chose an interdisciplinary faculty from the schools of sociology, law, business administration and engineering and they were placed on joint appointment in our programme. The head of the Los Angeles City Planning Department joined the faculty as well, on a part-time appointment to the studio. I was in charge of planning the studio, conducting it and directing and coordinating all their efforts.

I chose as our problem the re-design of the Santa Monica shore line and set about organising the lectures required from the studio faculty members and placing reading materials in the library. I wrote the book of philosophy, information and individual work topics, taking care to go no further, initially, than the second work programme. I had learned it was better to wait until I knew the students before structuring too much of their work.

International students

I was pleased I had waited. The students turned out to be an extremely mixed group. Many were from Europe. Two I taught in Italian the first semester and those from Germany had to make out as best they could with a dictionary. I saw their puzzlement; and tension as they encountered American culture and education, the same experience I had had as a foreign student but magnified by their lack of English. I remember the look of pained sorrow on the German students' faces as my assistant, Francis Ventre, announced 'Now I'm going to give you the break-out on the housing starts'. Hearing the sound of flying dictionary pages, I would often interrupt a lecturer by saying 'I'm afraid some of us haven't understood'. One Italian student, Margherita Paulis, who became our good friend, would sidle up to me and whisper of some faculty member 'Denise! He is *very* American!' This too would be a signal to me to warn the person concerned that he was not being understood.

My European students reacted as I had first done, from a background of CIAM urbanism and from cities where planning is dominated by civil servants. 'But what are people *doing* about Los Angeles?' asked one student, after our first visit to the Los Angeles City Planning Department. I should have guessed sooner than I did what he meant. He meant 'Where is that garret containing a team of young architects producing plans to convert Los Angeles into a megastructure?'

I remembered the end of my first semester at Penn when, after months of talk in our housing course, learning unfamiliar acronyms and digesting strange statistics, I finally realised that all the talk and all the figures suggested no remedy, but masked the scandal that Americans with houses don't care about those who don't have them. 'But what are you going to *do*?' I asked. 'I don't know', said Wheaton, doyen of housers, walker of Washington corridors, drafter of legislation: 'What are *you* going to do?'

I found the UCLA students difficult to teach. This was partly because they had not come to UCLA with definite expectations of what they were going to learn and they had not chosen the school because they believed in its educational stance. This was a different situation from the one at Penn, where students, particularly in the end, had come for Lou Kahn and for the social planners. In addition, there wasn't a backup from other faculty members who shared a profession and a school of thought.

Interdisciplinary education

My interdisciplinary faculty at UCLA were not planners. This meant that they did not express the troublesome scepticism and hostility toward architecture that frustrated my teaching at Penn. On the other hand they were not nearly as knowledgeable about urbanism. I had to be ready to shift throughout the semester as it became apparent who could do what among the interdisciplinary faculty. For example, I discovered that to the urban land economist, the term 'land' in the name of his field was unimportant. He was interested in money flows, not in the spatial economy. But I found one of his doctoral students who could and would give our students the down-to-earth basics of urban land economics that they needed to be urban designers. And to tell the truth, the students understood him better than they had his professor.

I had to plan many of my colleagues' lectures for them and indeed, to work equal time with them on the preparation of all lectures. This was extremely taxing. But it was necessary because few academics know what professionals need and non-architects usually cannot re-formulate their subject matter to derive its physical implications.

Shortly after this experience at UCLA, interdisciplinary education became first a byword and then a cuss word in architectural education. I am convinced that it fell into disrepute because the architecture faculty were unaware of how much effort they had to expend in preparing an interdisciplinary studio. Without this effort and the hardship of negotiating their positions with all faculty members, interdisciplinary studies are a waste of time.

Looking back on the FFF studios I taught at Penn and UCLA, I feel now that they were probably too rigidly organised and too comprehensive. They tried to cover too many disciplines and to cover them too completely. They could have been much looser and less ambitious. Something more partial might have been more lively and more educational for design students. My own inexperience made me want to be responsible for too much material. By stressing content so strongly, I helped open my students' eyes and minds to the richness of the urban designers' world, but left little time to help them polish their design skills.

Despite the requirement that they have 'particular design ability', few of the students who came out of the Penn or UCLA urban design programmes have remained designers or have exerted design influence through their work. Many have become good administrators and the heads of departments, agencies or firms. Perhaps they were turned in this direction in any case and it is noticeable that few urban designers anywhere have exerted design leadership or influenced the philosophy of urbanism or architecture. This suggests a question: is urban design education the best education for talented urban designers? To put it another way, what did these programmes train the students for? Charles Eames hired two of my urban design students. He found them 'extremely mature' and broadly based. He used them for movie-making and for researching the content of exhibitions.

Determinants of urban form
While at UCLA, I was trying to write a book. It was called *The Determinants of Urban Form* and I considered it, like my studios, to be primarily an aid to urban designers who must comprehend and find their own approach, as designers, to more material than is covered in architectural curricula.

In writing this book, I benefited from the insights of another friend and colleague, Charles Seeger, ethnomusicologist, founder of the field of ethnomusicology and Professor Emeritus, in his late 70s, in the School of Ethnomusicology at UCLA. Charles was doing for music ('musics' as he preferred to say) what I was trying to do for architecture and urban form. He endeavoured to comprehend music as a system of art and communication that is influenced by society and to describe it using another system of communication, language, that does not entirely do the job. Charles' taxonomies and his world's view, that included music, speech and my field (under 'artifacture') informed my attempt to define my own. His scholarly mastery of his field and his openness to all music, including popular music, I could compare with those of Gans and Venturi. While my students puzzled over my slides of Las Vegas, smirked on our visit to Disneyland and resolutely photographed only highways and bridges, not signs and not small houses, Charles happily shared my aesthetic experiences with me.

The book is unfinished. It was never funded. The social science foundations said 'Interesting but not our field'. The architectural ones said 'Wonderful but we have no money'.

Three studios at Yale
A year later I was back in Philadelphia, working with my second husband, Robert Venturi, and teaching with him at Yale. We taught three studios there. Though they were not urban design studios, they took an architectural view of urbanism and an urban view of architecture. They were definitely for designers. They used the format and pedagogical method of my planning and urban design studios, but were much looser affairs, that did not attempt such global syntheses and were tuned more to broadening the perspectives of would-be architects than to training urban designers. They were distinct departures from the typical architecture studio. First, their subjects were unusual. Their primary focus was architectural symbolism, which was investigated by the design of a subway station and the analysis of the suburban landscape. Second, they took up a major portion, almost all, of the students' semester credits. Third, they were interdisciplinary in subject matter, although most of the students were architects and the work they did was mainly architectural; the interdisciplinary education took the form of lectures and library work. Fourth, two were research rather than design studios. All included a research phases that were highly structured and that took place partly in the library and partly in the field.

Holmes Perkins had always impressed upon his planning faculty that design was the civic design students' first love and that they should not be called upon to move very far from it into boring research. With this in mind, when we returned from our ten days in Las Vegas, with our material ready for documenting and analysing, I scheduled a four-day sketch design, just to keep the students' architectural juices flowing. They described it as 'that busy-work Denise is getting us to do.' I think the key to involving architectural students in research is that the subject matter should be interesting to the students and connected with their needs as designers. For students in the tumultuous 1960s (Yale's architecture building burned just before our Levittown studio began) the subject matter had to be both iconoclastic and socially concerned. For such students, the casinos of Las Vegas and the houses of Levittown were certainly suitably iconoclastic choices. The shotgun marriage we made between this subject matter and social issues was a justifiable and convincing one for the times, although few architectural critics have understood that there could indeed be a socially concerned way of viewing commercial and suburban iconography. I have explained this connection elsewhere.

Within the overall subject matter, the aim was to give the students the equivalent of four courses in related topics. These ranged from cultural anthropology to regional science, from iconography to the structure of the home building industry. Remembering how easy it had been for urban design students to leave their design skills unhoned even as we discussed the relation of everything to design, we tried hard in these studios to find good architectural methods of relating analysis and design. To do so, we re-invented formal analysis. Others had invented it before us, but we applied it to the everyday landscape, using it as a means to avoid de-skilling designers and pointing out that the analysis of forms was suitable research for architects and urban designers.

We tried to stress that design could be interdisciplinary too. The design project for the Levittown studio gave the students four alternatives: to design a regional strategy for housing for the New Haven region; to design new roles for architects; to design low income, multi-family housing prototypes, suitable for insertion into existing suburban residential areas; and one project merely said, 'Do for housing what Oldenburg did for hamburgers.'

Our Yale studios led to publications and became well-known. They culminated my first decade of experience with studio education. They were for architecture students, but by the late 1960s graduate architecture students at Yale were much more sophisticated than had been their counterparts entering civic design at Penn in the early 60s. They approached urban design problems in the way I would like to see urban design students approach them.

I think these studios suggest a prototype for innovation of studio in architecture as well as in urban design. There are many individual buildings that can be treated in the same way, with research phases, group work and interdisciplinary juries. But they should not become the norm for all studio experience. In a professional programme, no architecture student should have more than one primarily research based studio and probably no urban design student either.

Rice studio
We ran a small urban design studio, at Rice University in 1967. It was an analysis of and an essay in aesthetic controls. The class was made up of third-year and fifth-year architecture students. We named the fifth-year students urban designers and the third-year students architects. We chose Westheimer Avenue in Houston, which started at the centre of the city and moved out to the suburbs, changing its character as it went, but retaining predominantly commercial and low rise multi-family housing uses along most of its length. We divided this street into seven different sections and asked the 'urban designers' to set up aesthetic controls for each section, based on its predominant character and land uses. These controls were not required to be of overwhelming rationality, as controls seldom are. One group decided that the style of new buildings in their area should be Spanish Colonial. Another removed car access to the commercial uses on Westheimer to expedite traffic flow and neaten up the sidewalks. The architects were required to respond to these controls with designs for the area. Then the urban designers altered their controls based on their experience of seeing them used. Then the architects designed yet again.

The intention was to test the controls by pushing them to extremes. Therefore, the architects were told to do their worst, not their best. This had an unexpected pedagogical windfall: the students became much more creative. It seemed that when the worst was to happen, they could forget their fears and inhibitions. Students exploited nooks and crannies in the sign legislation to create enormous blinking signs that betrayed the aesthetic intent of the controls while they followed the letter of the law. The requirement for Spanish styling, because the first time round the urban designers omitted the word 'Colonial', produced a Gaudiesque fantasy.

A further emphasis in this studio, as in all the others, was on the evolution of new graphic techniques suitable to new problems. This focus increases in importance as the philosophical stance of urban design shifts away from 'total design' and toward orchestration. For example, how do you indicate graphically that portions of the city will be built by the public sector and other portions by the private sector? How do you depict, on one plan, areas where an action is to be promoted and others where a reaction is expected? How do you differentiate between an intention and an expectation? How do you reveal the atomistic and fractionated uses and ownership of a small-scale, downtown commercial area, when the standard notation for commerce is just plain red ? How do you suggest the importance of signs in a landscape when they show up hardly at all on orthogonal projection?

In 1970, after the Levittown studio, Bob and I retired from academic life. We have continued to lecture and teach infrequently and act intermittently as advisors on architectural pedagogy. From 1973 to 1983 I was an advisor to the Departments of Architecture and Urban Planning at MIT and more recently to the Department of Architecture at Temple University. In 1983 I taught another studio at Penn on (roughly) the sociology and symbolism of park landscapes; and in 1989 one at Harvard a (roughly) public and private, fact and value, in the architecture of emerging institutions. For a few years I kept my hand in in moral education, 1960s-style, by serving on the curriculum committee of the Jewish Children's Folkshul in Philadelphia. Perhaps the rip-roaring atmosphere around planning juries and the Theory of Planning seminar at Penn in the early 1960s resembled, more than the discourse of Socrates, the *pilpul* of an eastern European *yeshiva*. Urban design education could do with some of this atmosphere.

Questions and answers

With my point of departure clarified, I can draw conclusions. In so doing, I shall re-state my position, now, not as personal history, but as pedagogical theory and principle. I shall do this by attempting to answer the questions set in the agenda for an urban design educators' retreat, for which this paper was originally written.

How are existing urban design programmes constituted?
I have described several urban design programmes I have known and have also tried to show how they changed over time. Schools should change to stay relevant to their societies. However, planners of urban design programmes should watch these swings and not act on the last year's or the last decade's clarion call.

What are the limits to the field's concerns?
Urban designers are called planners by architects and architects by planners. This retreat and these questions are demonstrations that there is a considerable identity crisis in the field and there has been since the 1960s.

My own personal definitions, which respond to my own interests and the experiences of my career, may prove too broad for many urban designers. I call myself an architect and planner and see my involvement in urban design as a focus within this broader spectrum. Architecture is the window through which I view my world, personal and professional. The span between architecture and planning – and then some – is the range of concerns that I bring to my work. Urban design is a type of design I do or am involved in. This is not a question of scale but of approach. An urbanistic approach would inform my criticism of the partitions in an office space, a health systems plan, an economic development plan, or even the proportions of a teapot. I have used concepts derived from transportation planning to suggest an approach to the design of academic classroom buildings. Involvement in advocacy planning has converted me to a user advocate for architectural users; for example, for the rights of secretaries to have natural light.

'Way of life' and 'quality of life' are concepts that interest urban designers. I feel they apply as well to individual buildings. I like to share in evolving the basic *parti* of our architectural projects, where my role is to help arrive at the 'what', as Kahn called it. To me this means creatively defining the way (or ways) of life of the building and designing or foreseeing situations that its physical facilities and their configuration must accommodate or may evoke.

The breadth of my approach to urban design is probaby too costly for most urban budgets, yet the shift from architecture to urban design should entail a broadening of scope. When urban designers limit their field of vision too much, their plans become dead, irrelevant and coercive.

Perhaps in defining urban design we should discuss its essence rather than its limits. For me, the essence of the urban design approach is that it concentrates more on relations between objects, more on linkages, contexts and in between places, than on the objects themselves. It deals with long time-spans, incremental growth over time, decision-making that is complex and fractionated and relations between different levels and types of decision-making. Urban design is the subtle organisation of complexity, the orchestration of sometimes inharmonious instruments, the awareness that discord at a certain level can be resolved as harmony at another. It requires patience. It is a pinpoint upon which it is difficult for the professional to live. Many urban designers go 'back' to architecture and others go 'back' to planning.

Put a group of architects, urban designers and planners in a sightseeing bus and their actions will define the limits of their concerns. The architects will take photographs of buildings or highways or bridges. The urban designers will wait for that moment when the three are juxtaposed. The planners will be too busy talking to look out of the window.

Are there tendencies towards sub-specialisation within urban design education?
Thrusts toward specialisation exist, and they relate to historical cycles in urban development. Community design as practiced by most urban designers probably had its genesis in the advocacy planning movement of the 1960s. Urban conservation and environmental quality design belong with the ecology movement and the trend toward historicism in the 1970s. Urban development design is what is left of the urban design practices of the 1950s. It is most in need of regeneration for today. (That was written in 1981. This has been, for good or ill, the area of urban design most influenced by 1980s Post-Modernism.)

Although I believe urban design is an approach rather than a geographic boundary, there is truth to the claim that urban designers who work in the private sector, the planning agency, or the re-development authority, should take positions related to their location. Consultant urban designers should take different positions from agency urban designers. Whether these should be educational specialisations or occupational deformations is open to question. However, schools of urban design should differ from each other in order to diversify educational opportunities to suit different students. A valid basis for differentiation can be the nature of the institution within which the programme is housed. Urban design education at MIT should be different from that at UCLA, for more reasons that I can list here. Of course, they should each give basics needed to qualify the student in the field and these should be discussion on what such basics are. But urban design in particular, because it is such an interdisciplinary field, should relate its offerings to the strengths of its institution, stressing social concern in one school, historical preservation in another and engineering rigour in a third. Urban design programmes should move with the times, regarding not only social questions and technology, but also theories and principles of the field. Urban designers have been particularly slow to catch up with changes in theory in both architecture and planning. They are generally behind the times, when they should be the most up front. Little good theory and little intellectual and design leadership has come from the urban design community, academic or professional.

Should current curriculums emphasise professionalism or scholarship?
I believe they should emphasise scholarship. I myself am more interested in professional education and its philosophy than in academic education and feel this is by far the most exciting form of education for a professional to be involved in. However, professional education requires the conversion of academic scholarship for purposes of action and I believe that at the moment we have insufficient academic scholarship in urban design to convert. We haven't even managed to convert the writings of other disciplines to suit our purposes. We've left it to the architects and planners to do this for us and of course they do it from their own point of view.

I think great schools of urban design should stress philosophy, but it should be the philosophy of action. They should stress it a little too much, leaving their bright students to flounder and struggle in their first years out of school, but well equipped to survive in the twentieth and thirtieth years of their careers. The floundering will be a challenge in any case, though it is hard on their employers.

Are our teaching methods (eg reliance on studio models) in need of an overhaul?
If urban design education were to drop studio now, it would at last catch up with the 1960s. This would demonstrate what I mean about urban designers following trends at too great a distance. 'Learning by doing', is an integral part of most professional education. Planning schools should not have given it up in the first place. But, as I have tried to suggest throughout this paper, studio needs to be overhauled and made much more demanding, on both faculty and students, to be suitable to graduate professional education in urban design and architecture.

The need for analytic teaching and research does not diminish the need for studio. In fact, studio is a suitable vehicle for much of this type of teaching. Grand interdisciplinary, research-based studios can be a wonderful introduction for incoming urban design students to the full scope of their new field. However, for advanced, independent students headed toward the doctorate, studio can prove a limitation from which they should be freed.

Most urban design studios should be highly structured. This means urban design professors should spend portions of their summers preparing for their studios. Most academics teach the same thing over and over again, more or less. When they want to change their subject matter, they get money to do so over the summer. Studio faculty should get such money every year. Schools of urban design should learn about the academic category 'preparation materials'. It's a source of funding for studio.

Some people worry that highly structured studios will be limiting to the creativity of students. I have rarely heard such worries from students in the studios themselves, particularly when the subject matter is challenging and new to them. This fear is often voiced, however, by other faculty members viewing the project from outside. There are many ways to structure a studio to challenge and not limit the creativity of students. One way is to plan ahead no more than ten days at a time. This lets one see which way the students' interest is going and help to direct it. It allows options and choices of subject matter all the way along. A well-structured studio helps students understand the overall process of planning as well as everyone else's role in it. It is an invaluable aid to them in their future careers, particularly if they are to become educators. And no matter how much the studio is structured by the studio critic in the beginning, by the end the students should be doing the structuring for themselves. If it is well done in the beginning, the students will have learned to do it by the end.

What skills should a graduate urban designer have? What roles are we training people for?
It would be a major achievement if urban design education could make designers aware that there *are* different design roles in the city. Idealistic European architects believe they plan for the people. Sceptical designers should know that plans are made for the people who pay for them. This is not nice but true. Only urban designers who understand it will be able to slip through the cracks and plan according to their social concerns.

I don't have answers to these questions but I do have some of my own questions: To what extent do the skills required for the different roles differ? Is there an overlap? Should there be a core curriculum suitable for all urban designers? Should this core be shared with architects and urban planners? Should urban designers receive mainly the common core and find their focus and specialisation in practice?

Who can be an urban designer?
I myself believe that training *and experience* in architecture should be a prerequisite for urban design study. On the other hand, I think all architects and planners should receive rudimentary education in urban design as part of their introduction to their field. (Some architecture courses go too far in the other direction, they give so many 'urban design' – in actuality large-scale architecture – projects that the students of architecture don't learn skills.) At the end of the first professional programme, that is, the architecture programme, there should be the opportunity to begin to specialise in urban design as well as in other fields, say for the last semester.

Can a case be made that urban design is becoming an identifiable discipline rather than a field of studies?
No I don't think so. For me, urban design still lacks what constitutes a 'discipline' – a penumbra of scholarship, theory and principles, a set of generally recognised working methods, an institutional setting and a mass of practitioners. To me, the proper location for most schools of urban design is within a strong architecture programme. Then, the urban designers should be kept in creative and even painful tension between this programme and a sceptical, critical, social sciences-based department of urban planning. Students should enter such an urban design programme with degrees in either architecture or landscape architecture and, preferably, with study travel and a couple of years of practice behind them.

THE PUBLIC REALM

The Public Sector And The Public Interest In Urban Design

Urban designers, whether they work in public agencies or the private sector, must have a philosophy of the relation between public and private in the city. At the turn of the century, city planning in America meant civic planning. Planners and designers of the City Beautiful movement focused their attention on the public ceremonial parts of the city and Beaux-Arts schools of architecture offered programmes in 'civic design'. Daniel Burnham's plan for Chicago, the civic design plan par excellence, contained recommendations for all city areas controlled by city government, for roads, parks, the subway, the waterfront and the World's Fair site. Although we remember the public images of this plan, as noteworthy were its strategic approach and system-wide scope. In it, the public realm of Chicago was shown as a set of linked networks overlaid on the metropolis. Within this filament, public buildings were placed at important junctions and rendered in Beaux-Arts splendour, private buildings were limned impressionistically to suggest an intersitial fabric.

The Great Depression of the 1920s and 1930s changed planners' views of the public role in urbanism. Under the New Deal, government aid to cities was primarily economic and social and was rendered through existing and invented economic procedures. Where aid was physical, it was in the service of economic and social aims; dams were built to promote rural electrification, public housing was sponsored to improve the condition of the poor and new towns were initiated as beacons toward the good life.

The New Deal brought other levels of government into the affairs of the city, particularly the federal government. Federal 'pump-priming' had its origin in the 1930s. However, its effect on urban and suburban growth was felt most strongly after World War II, with the returning veterans and the mass migrations of rural southerners to northern cities. In the 1950s and 1960s the federal government was heavily involved in urban development. Federal measures typically encouraged the private sector to meet the pent-up post-war demand for building. Public sector mechanisms evolved for doing so were both indirect (for example, mortgage programmes for suburban housing) and direct (the acquiring and consolidating of decayed urban property for re-sale to private developers). After the federal urban renewal legislation of the 1940s and 1950s, planning was no longer solely the affair of city government, nor was its scope limited by the city boundary. This led to re-definitions in the field and, during the 1960s, university departments of city planning changed their names to 'city and regional' or simply 'urban' planning.

In architecture, the young idealists of the Modern movement had, since the 1920s, complained that the design of civic ceremonial spaces was a socially worthless task and that the architect's province should be the whole city, public and private, but with emphasis on 'social housing', the housing for the poor. Urban designers of the Modern movement saw government as the purveyor of social good; indeed, the European urban visions, of the 1920s, which served as models for designers in both Europe and America, presumed government was the major and perhaps the only client for urban design. In the 1950s the federal government brought Modern architecture with it into the American city and 'civic design' was re-named 'urban design'. However, much Modern movement urbanism was, in fact, architecture at large scale. Modern architects in Europe and America approached the design of the city as they would the design of a building for a single client; the same measure of control was to be applied across the board – to a neighbourhood, a single house, an individual unit within a megastructure, a roadway, a public space, or a park bench. Burnham had understood his role as a strategist and orchestrator of many designers on the urban design scene; the Modernists did not.

Some definitions

Urban design's span over the design decisions of many unassociated people defines one of its major differences from architecture. Procedurally, the difference between architecture and urban design turns more upon differences in responsibility for designing and implementing than upon differences of size or scale. Also important is time. Urban design must encompass the flower that will bloom tomorrow and an expressway that will last a thousand years. Although the largest part of urban design work fits within time scales similar to those of architecture, the urban design spectrum expands beyond in both directions. The element of continuity, too, is different. The urban designer must consider generations of use and re-use of the urban fabric, beyond the initial programme of the first client. However, the urban designer's approach to the time dimension can, and usually should, be applied to architecture as well.

The notion of *the public sector* probably derives from economics. The urban public sector consists of governmental agencies, at all levels, that are involved in the functioning of metropolitan areas. Semi-public agencies, some private institutions and private citizens in some aspect of their lives, can be considered part of the public sector as well.

I define *the public realm* as the public sector seen in physical terms. We may view the public realm simple-mindedly as everything on the city transportation plan and everything that is blue or green on the city land use map. Strict constructionists may complain that this includes churches and private schools in the public realm; yet in all cities there are private places that feel more 'public' than many public places: John Wanamaker's eagle in Philadelphia, the Peabody Hotel fountain in Memphis, Main Street in Disneyland and the interior of Quincy Market in Boston, are examples of such private-public places. Nolli's famous map of 18th-century Rome gives an illuminating definition of the public realm and of its relation to the private city.

All buildings have their public aspects: in a house, the front door and the parlour; in an office building, the entry and lobby; in a museum, the lobby and main stairway and so on. There is a progression from public to private through most private buildings and there is an important 'in-between' realm, as Aldo Van Eyck called it, between public and private – building facades are the primary urban in-between realm and a major interest of urban design.

Within the public realm itself, a differentiation can be made between *public* and *civic*. Mark Lilla defines public places as those, like the shopping mall, marketplace and beach, that 'serve our shared but still private needs' whereas civic places are where we 'share places and purposes', by virtue of sharing citizenship.[1] In the one, he says, we take our private enjoyment in public, in the other, we act civilly and perhaps ceremoniously. Civic places are those of government, such as city hall and its courtyard, but also the museum and concert hall where we share a citizenship of the world. The civic can be found, as well, in the private – in, for example, the proudly discreet front door of a townhouse. And there is little relation between civic and size, a quite small building can be civic.

Civic design covers the ceremonial or institutional aspects of the public realm, whereas *urban design* covers the whole city. Both have a long-range time dimension but in civic design the responsibility for design, implementation and maintenance is assigned to a single group or small number of groups, whereas in urban design the responsibility is broadly based. Civic design projects are typically designed for, built by, and maintained by the public sector, civic groups, or a combination of both.

Some private or semi-public institutions can be *affected with the public interest*. This legal concept, which justifies the regulation of telephone and taxi companies, can justify applying special controls to portions of the private realm that may be of particular importance to the public.

A further term of interest is the *commons*. This is land over which different members of the community have different rights: some to cross it, others to graze it, yet others to cultivate it or gather its brushwood. Although pre-industrial societies have commons, modern US examples are hard to find. Perhaps some type of commons exists in fact, though not in law, where city residents cultivate crops on abandoned urban lots.

The scope of these terms is narrower than the broad topic of architecture and society, yet broader than the special issues of social concern in architecture and public participation in community design. Care for the public realm in cities may or may not be equated with social or democratic ideals. In designs commissioned by despots, it frequently is not. Of course it should be. Methods of involving the community democratically in urban decision-making are discussed elsewhere in this book. Here the aim is to survey the part played by the professional rather than the community, and to discuss the urban designer's role in relation to specific portions of the city, various methods of implementing design ideas and the roles of others in the urban polity.

In the task of bridging the gap between architecture and social need, the public realm may not be the most directly relevant subject to ponder, neither will the needed swing of the architectural pendulum toward social concern be achieved by architects' returning to the well-intended but mistaken belief that the world can be saved by good design. Nevertheless, a discussion of the public aspects of urban design could be one step on the way toward re-uniting architectural and social thought.

The relation between public and private
The definition of what is public and what is private varies from culture to culture and over time within one culture. For example, there are public ovens in the villages of some societies; for most cultures, education is a public or group undertaking; and in United States cities public toilets have migrated to the private sector, where they are found in department stores and gasoline stations but rarely elsewhere.

Shifts in the relation between public and private occur in response to changing social and economic conditions and the changing demands people make on cities. In the American city before World War II, streets were predominantly public and buildings mainly private. Public buildings were those used for government, education, religion (*pace* the US constitution) and defence. Although by the 20th century these were no longer the largest buildings in town, they tended to be among the most solidly built and were designed to last. Public buildings had a civic look but, apart from Philadelphia's city hall and the

occasional state capitol, there were no set locations for public buildings in the American city, as there were in the European city.

During the first three post-war decades, government-sponsored urban renewal changed the nature of the public realm and increased its visibility. Federal programmes broke the traditional relation between public and private in cities. The *Ville Radieuse*-type urban renewal projects that altered the face of the American city were joint ventures between agencies of government and the private sector. In them, buildings no longer lined streets but stood apart in open spaces (frequently parking lots) and it was unclear where the public ended and the private began. In the 1970s and 1980s, downtown malls and atriums, borrowed from the suburbs, were publicly sponsored and used but privately owned. Yet even at the height of government support of city-building the private realm continued to predominate and John Kenneth Galbraith, writing in the late 1950s, could castigate an America where private affluence and public squalor were combined.[2] During this period, the urban freeway system became the most highly visible part of the public realm and remains so today.

The 1970s and 1980s brought political conservatism and a reduction in government spending on urbanism. With federal funds diminished, city agencies sought methods of leveraging small investments of public money to generate large expenditures of private funds. Strategies of action and reaction between the public and private sectors were refined. The investment tax credit for the renewal of old and historic buildings was one such effort to induce private sector investment without direct expenditure of public funds.

In today's city, it is inevitable that there will be more private buildings than public buildings, but should the private dominate? The extent to which they do will vary for Washington DC and the Las Vegas Strip. In 1900, public sidewalks in Philadelphia's Old City consisted of slabs of granite 15 feet long and 10 feet wide. Today, in Las Vegas, the private sector can erect a neon sign 22 stories high. The public sector role in Las Vegas is mainly regulatory. (This is no small contribution: for example, the county's parking requirements have largely dictated the shape of the famous Strip.) The public sector's own contribution to the physical order of the Strip – the sidewalks, medians, streets, street signs and traffic lights – are modest indeed, although not non-existent. Public Philadelphia, too, can no longer afford granite curbstones, let alone sidewalks, but the private sector has erected 'public-private' spaces such as The Gallery shopping mall and the lobby of One Liberty Place, an office building. The erection of this building was much contested because it rises above the height of William Penn's hat at the top of the city hall tower. With it, the issue of private versus public dominance arose literally in stark silhouette on the Philadelphia skyline.

Broad scale civic projects are seldom built today. This is in part owing to government's straightened circumstances but it is also because civic design processes are not set up to deal with the pluralism of the modern city. Grand civic gestures can be easily vitiated by powerful interest groups that disagree with their aims. Even projects with multiple sponsors may fail in the rough and tumble of urban power-broking, partly because many of the most worthy groups have formed a distrust of the good intentions of government. Where civic design succeeds it is usually because it is sponsored by a civic organization that operates as watch-dog, implementer, funder, maintainer, and supporter of the project and because this group has convinced the city that its project is in the interest of the whole community. In this case the group's design will probably also be accepted. Such projects are likely to be single buildings, for example a museum or a concert hall. Even then, conflicting interests may have to be satisfied or quieted. It's merely easier to do so when the building is not large.

When extensive downtown improvements or large civic complexes, such as convention centres, are sponsored and executed by government, they are usually promoted by powerful private groups to serve their own economic interest. Government expedites and provides the coordination the group needs; construction costs and maintenance can then be financed from the economic returns such projects bring or may be paid for through taxes, tax increment financing and special assessments on the private sector. This is another example of public-private co-ordination and to that extent, has more to do with urban design than civic design. Or is it the private sector posturing as government?

Another recent shift in the public-private balance has been engineered by business groups that sponsor downtown arts districts to provide a public anchorage for private development. In some cities developers have felt public plans were lacking or inadequate and have hired private planning consultants, hoping to convince the city to adopt their recommendations in the interest of maintaining value and amenity. In such private takeovers of the public role the question arises whether there should not be, beyond the ubiquitous transportation systems, some irreducible minimum of public purpose that is maintained by the public. This question even more seriously concerns low-income and moderate-income housing: what is the federal 'safety net' in public housing? If government will not take responsibility for this housing, who will?

Public sector strategies for the public and private city

American urban planners tend to see themselves as strategists whose role is to recommend policy to urban decision-makers. To plan, in this model, is to intervene in an on-going, multivalent set of urban processes, working the art of the possible and using finely-tuned instruments to head toward an ideal but shifting vision of the future.

Planning guidance in American cities is exerted through a series of legal powers and administrative arrangements that enable and regulate urban development. Planning, subdivision and zoning regulations allow planners to guide and check the private sector. Their strategic role (where they still have one) in the formulation of urban capital programmes and budgets, lends planners the power of suasion in guiding the building decisions of city agencies such as school districts and departments of parks and recreation.

Although the private sector supplies the major source of funds for urban building, funding comes as well from the public sector. Changes in goals or in prevailing philosophies may direct public funding toward different local problems and various agencies. Neighbourhood improvements will be made when local communities receive loans and grants, transit malls will be built when Congress mandates mass transit funding and historical buildings will be preserved when an investment tax credit is allowed on their renovation. The urban planning function itself shifts its location as the sources of funding shift: from the city planning department, to the housing and community agency, to the semi-public commission and to private development offices. Planners migrate where the money is.

Urban designers have tended to place themselves above the morass, planning for a subjectively defined 'good of the people'. The 'good' may be architectural qualities such as 'urbanity', 'identity', or 'human scale'. Architectural planning for the city has stressed the visionary. Some architectural visions, for example, *Ville Radieuse* and Broadacre City, have profoundly influenced today's urbanism, purely through their power as published images. But in the daily life of urban development, architect's plans tend to be ineffective, despite their honourable intentions, because they are insufficiently tied to accepted methods of making and implementing urban decisions. Urban designers, whether in the public or private sector, should, for the most part, share with planners a philosophy of producing the best of the possible within the matrix of the available. Urban aesthetic aims and physical designs must depend for their implementation on current legal and institutional mechanisms for city building, and urban designers must devise strategies for the best use of these mechanisms.

In a pair of seminal essays written in the 1960s, David Crane considered what such urban design strategies might be.[3] He observed that in today's pluralistic 'city of a thousand designers', the urban designers' role is to guide the design decisions of many others in both the public and the private sectors. He likened the urban design process to painting on a river: adding to what was already flowing, seeing the new colours blend with others and the sharp outlines blurred by the flow. He pointed out that urban planners, through their role in capital programming and in highway and street design, could establish some form of control over almost 50 percent of the physical city. There should be, he argued, a *capital design* to go with the capital programme. This capital design would produce a *capital web* within which private sector building could be slung. If the web were strong and dominant, the private sector could be allowed greater design freedom than now exists through zoning and other controls. The public sector would be what was visible.

This vision of direct design control of the public realm and control at one remove of the private sector was an outcome of the strong presence of the federal government in urban development at that time. Unfortunately, even in the 1960s this formulation was too simple. Agencies of government did not and do not co-operate with each other any more easily than they get together with the private sector. In fact, relationships between arts districts and developers may be easier to formulate than those between city planners and transportation engineers. Later, when federal support for cities diminished, it was inconceivable that public improvements built by government could dominate in any except the most civic areas. So other types of strategy, perhaps less system-wide and more mixed, became necessary for the era of Nixon and Reagan. But the concept of urban design as an intervention in an on-going flow of designs and projects, that works through guidance and orchestration of the decisions of many others and that enlists all available planning resources, both public and private, is an important one.

Some public sector strategies used today in urban design implementation strategies today are:
Legal mechanisms such as official plans, zoning and subdivision controls. These tools of planning and the design standards they promulgate shape not only the broad bulk and mass of urban buildings but often the architectural character of details, surfaces and proportions. Design control, for better or worse, may be exercised at various points in the legal approval processes, as projects are scrutinized by different government agencies.
Public sector construction and maintenance. Though the notion of the capital web may be too far-reaching for most cities, the public infrastructure of the city is the great urban builder. The street system, as Crane claimed, is the major determinant of urban form. The architecture of public projects can serve as a good example to guide local aesthetic decisions and public buildings can act as anchors and initiators for the private sector. The level of physical maintenance of the public sector will affect private building decisions and influence private building maintenance.
Design review. Public sector review of designs produced by architects is a widely accepted method of achieving aesthetic aims. This review, conducted during the design process, may be

quantitative – a mechanistic assessment by agency staff of whether numerical constraints upon height, width, set-back or overhang have been met– or it may be qualitative and embody some chosen group's judgement on whether 'good' has been achieved. Opportunities to exercise design review exist within many of the procedures of city planning and in most cities design review is exercised by several bodies, including design review boards, re-development authorities, historical commissions, departments of licenses and inspections and planning staffs. Although design review is frequently ineffective and may be subject to abuse, it is the method of choice of an ever-increasing number of cities.

Illustrated design guidelines. These clarify the intentions of the plan and explain the reasoning and theory behind the urban design recommendations. If design guidelines are well done, they can, in my opinion, be more useful than design review as a means of communication between urban designers in the public sector and their architect colleagues in the agencies and the private sector.

Suasion. Within this category belong public agency activities such as sharing information, giving or taking design advice, jawboning and discussing design issues at community and interest-group meetings. Although the formal outcome of these may be a planning document with legal status, the informal results – the development of joint understanding and shared intentions, the evolving of methods of interaction – may be more important than the document itself in ensuring the success of the plan.

Moving from well-intentioned aspirations and prescriptions to implementable public policies and the means of implementing them is particulary difficult in the area of aesthetics. This is not only because tastes differ, but because the area of taste is qualitative and undefinable; the same words can be used to design vastly different physical results and, in assaying the quality of these results, we are bound to depend on the discretion of judges to whom we have assigned the role of tasks experts. This discretionary system, 'rule by man', rather than 'rule by law', must be protected carefully by constraints and gidelines as it can easily lead, as does absolute power in general, to corruption; or at least to taste coercion.

The design components of the public realm

The architectural character of the public realm will vary from city to city, for portions of a city and even for portions of a neighbourhood or street; and it will change with time. A range of options for the character of the different components of the realm should be considered by the urban designer.

Streets

Scarred by battles with community groups in the 1960s and 1970s, transportation engineers finally admitted urban designers to the project team. The urban designer is there to satisfy the communities by ensuring the 'good design' of new facilities and the conservation of neighbourhood values. The urban design task is often defined as suggesting ways to mitigate the effects of large engineering structures on neighbourhoods. Sometimes the 'mitigations' designed to satisfy environmental protection laws are high, concrete sound barriers that loom larger on the cityscape than the expressways they mitigate and are considerably uglier. Such measures disfigure the public realm to protect the private one.

At another level, calls for paving, curbing and street furniture designs are often made by planning agencies, because cities have funds for street improvements. However, if design for the public realm is to achieve more than cosmetics, urban designers' prescriptions for streets must go beyond mitigation and flower pots. What kind of street is the designer dealing with? Is it a tree-lined suburban way? A city street walled by townhouses? A parkway flanked by public buildings? An alley in a warehouse district? Or a retail arterial proposed for a transit way? Is it an expressway, a commercial strip, or an automobile row? Is it in a totally new area? Has it been defined as a special purpose street? What is the nature of its traffic? Is it closed to traffic? How does it accommodate pedestrians? What is its role in the urban circulation system? What is its intended future role? What is its role in the hierarchy of urban symbols?

How do buildings sit on this street? Has the nature of the relation to the sidewalk of front doors, store entrances, or building lobbies changed? What is the architectural character of buildings along this street? Are they unified or varied? Are there several discernible characters? Are there several scales? Are there typical materials or typical proportions of openings? Is there a dominant roof or cornice line? Do zoning regulations constrain street appearance? Do zoning incentives demand set-backs or piazzas that break the continuity of the street?

Should this street be primarily reticent and private, communicating that it belongs more to its locality than to the city at large, or should it be civic and welcoming of all who come? Should it permit signs and, if so, what type? Should it welcome trees? If it has become a truck route, should attempts at maintaining amenity be abandoned and its lateral users be encouraged to re-orient to their back entrances? If it is an expressway, can it be civic?

Public and Civic Buildings

The public sector urban designer may have a hand in siting an important public project, in locating its entry and service points and in controlling the stresses these may make on the surrounding urban fabric. Thereafter, the suasion process, through guidelines, works best. Because civic buildings are both the jewels in the public realm and the plums of private practice, the tension between architect and urban designer may intensify when they debate the architectural character of important civic buildings, or even of small public buildings. It is better that the first exchanges involve a comparison of the client's programme with the urban design guidelines, before the design is initiated, rather than a confrontation between the building's architect and the city's design review board after the *parti* is found.

The urban designer should be able to describe to the (often out-of-town) architect of an important public project the city's traditional methods of siting and designing civic buildings. Such information may, in itself, set the stage for continuity in architectural relationships. Beyond this, architects and urban designers should consider what distinguishes public architecture from private architecture.

All public institutional buildings, whether symbolically important or not, share a requirement for toughness and longevity, based on the intensity of their use, the numbers of people using them, the need for ease of maintenance and low operating costs and the fact that they will last beyond the lives of present users. These factors make institutional buildings look institutional. Most public sector buildings should be tough and gutsy; this quality distinguishes them from most private sector buildings, which may range from the rickety to the elegant, but seldom need to be as sturdy as public buildings.

For some public and civic buildings there is an added requirement to look monumental. Architects have traditionally borrowed from Classical imagery to achieve monumentality and there was a return to this method in the 1980s. However, buildings that are not Classical can be monumental through their formal qualities.[4] Monumental buildings tend to have simple, severe silhouettes. Within them are scale hierarchies derived from the need to admit and accommodate individuals and crowds. The soaring cathedral doorway within which a person-sized door is cut is an extreme example of scale combination. Juxtapositions between elements designed for small and large numbers of people make the large-scale elements seem larger and heighten the monumentality. Such juxtapositions are perhaps the essence of civic monumentality. Where the small scale is lacking, the large often looks scale-less and also unfriendly; this is one of the characteristics of architecture that is called 'fascist'. Monumentality relates only indirectly to the size of the building; it is a matter more of scale, and even small buildings can be monumental. Perhaps the best example of a small, civic building with monumental scale is the fire station. There are several reasons: fire stations must combine large doorways for fire trucks with domestic-sized windows and doors for the fire-fighters' living spaces. With truck and people-scaled elements juxtaposed in one small building, the designer can hardly miss. In addition, because fire stations are among the smallest of public buildings, they may be ones to risk on a young or controversial architect. This may account for the many distinguished 19th-century fire stations that are found in American cities.

Formal and abstract qualities may be less important to the public in the defining of civic monumentality than are symbols and metaphors. Fire stations may or may not still have towers, but it is a matter for comment when city halls don't. Where there is public expectancy that civic buildings look a certain way, design guidelines should deal with this expectation head-on. The reverse is the case for public housing. A public housing project should not look like 'a project'. The more public housing can merge with its surroundings, the happier will its residents be. However, the visual stigma of housing projects is a challenge to designers, not a reason for cities to abandon public housing.

Parks and Open Space
Departments of parks and recreation tend to see their charge as maintenance, acquisition, de-acquisition, community relations and providing recreation of the type people need, where they need it. Planning agencies see parks as community facilities and the destination points of 'journeys to recreation'. Community groups may define an intended park as a 'nimby' – a facility that is good in the abstract but 'not in my back yard'. Most landscape architects see parks as problems in recreational land use planning, land management, ecological preservation, architectural design and the finding of suitable plant materials. It is up to the urban designer to set the park, or the system of parks, in the urban and metropolitan context and to demonstrate the role of parks in the city's cultural landscape.

This requires an understanding of the historical relation between park development and the social philosophies and artistic fashions in vogue at the time of their initiation.[5] Urban design guidelines should define the historic and symbolic landscapes of the urban park system and should relate these, not only to the neighbourhoods in which they were developed, but to the cultures of their times, showing how parks give physical expression to the aspirations of the society. The different landscapes should be documented and analysed, setting out what is worth preserving as the system adjusts to meet new demands.

Ways in which today's philosophies and cultures continue to find expression in our parks should be brought to attention. A recent example is the development of park fitness trails for the jogging urbanites of the 1980s. The ecology and the historical preservation movements have both influenced recent park design and management and, historically, every form or urban transportation has routed its vehicles through urban parkways. An emerging form in American cities today is the downtown office

park, where workers from surrounding buildings go at lunch hour to sit, eat a sandwich, gaze at each other, meet in conversation and take their *passeggiata*.[6]

Public control over the private city
If most private buildings have a public face, what is the nature of the public's interest in this face? Should private buildings be 'background buildings' to the public sector? Always? What of 'private' projects built by the public, such as public housing? Should private building in historic districts be more controlled than private building elsewhere?

The public sector is concerned with private buildings to the extent that they are affected with the public interest and relate to the public realm. Therefore, the urban design plan should include recommendations on private buildings: on their uses, height and bulk, access to sun and light, entrances and exits, the privacy and safety they provide, and the enjoyment of their users. Traditional zoning controls direct the design of individual buildings in order to maintain these amenities (more correctly, zoning, as a police power, protects public health, safety and welfare, which have been deemed, by law, to include financial prosperity and aesthetic enjoyment). The urban designer should examine existing zoning legislation for its effect on overall architectural and urban design character and for its relevance to changing trends.

The relation between public and private designers assumed to exist by the zoning codes broke down with urban renewal. In order to attain public goals for the rebirth of cities, the federal urban renewal programme permits government to exercise its power to amass land, write down its cost and re-sell it to the private sector, in exchange for obtaining a greater than usual control over private decisions and designs. Urban renewal agencies produce 'indicative site plans' for both the public realm and private buildings, then agency planners vet private architects' attempts to follow the guidance of these plans while meeting the needs of their private clients.

A further re-definition of the public interest in private buildings occurred in the late 1960s, when private developers were allowed to increase the total building area of downtown projects if they incorporated elements for the public good in their buildings. The public good included plazas and non-economic uses such as theatres. In the 1970s, financial incentives (mainly tax breaks) were devised to induce private owners of historic buildings to cede rights in their property, especially in their facades, to the public in order to preserve them and maintain the integrity of important historic districts. In some cities owners of historically or architecturally valuable buildings were enabled to sell their development rights to abutting or nearby property owners in order to survive financially without sacrificing their buildings.

Another development has been 'aesthetic zoning', promulgated for cities once the courts had decided that the police powers could protect the visual environment. Now the traditional tussle between public and private designers over the building facade is extended to cover whole buildings, as for example in San Francisco, where a zoning code mandates Post-Modernism for high-rise office buildings.[7] Aesthetic zoning may define the silhouettes of high-rise buildings, or prescribe their articulation in plan, or require all downtown buildings to have storefronts at street level, or demand that all open spaces contain a specified percentage of 'green'.

Design controls exerted by the public sector over the private since the 1950s have, in my opinion, moved the responsibility for private design too far toward the public sector. There have been some unwanted results, for example, overcrowding or plazas the public does not need or cannot use. Some controls produce a sad deadening of the environment; by mandating standards of taste, the risk of bad architecture is reduced but blandness results. By suppressing the possibility for dialogue between the individual and the general, the opportunity to learn from the specific is missed and uniqueness is lost.

Nevertheless, public sector input in private building decisions is necessary. It should be exerted through the urban plan, through traditional zoning and planning controls, through the urban design plan and through design guidelines. Private architects and builders need to learn the city's view of the area in which they are building, preferably before they start designing. The urban design plan should show how the city sees its present architectural and symbolic character, what it is striving for and what the public sector can offer the individual project or building.

The public realm within the urban plan
Prescriptions for the public and private realms need to be made within the framework of an overall view of the city. City-wide planning that sets the context for other levels of planning is the responsibility of the public sector. It goes without saying that a good design for the public realm requires a realistic plan for the city, with a strong urban design component.

At the metropolitan scale the character of the city is defined by the largest elements of the public realm – topography, portions of the freeway network, intense centres of activity – as well as by important symbolic buildings and spaces. The Bay and the Golden Gate Bridge in San Francisco, the Mississippi River and the Bluffs in Memphis, the river and skyline in Manhattan, and Independence Hall and the Liberty Bell in Philadelphia are each part of its city's public realm. Although they range widely in size, each sets their stamp on a metropolis. This broadest level of the public realm must be considered at the scale of the overall plan. The plan also handles other metropolitan-wide elements – for example, the transportation system – and defines the relationship between   all elements.

The particular province of the urban design plan is to spell out connections and linkages between parts of the city at all scales, from the region to the individual building. Urban design may be defined as design of the connections between events or objects, rather than the events and objects themselves. Where the service access to an office building should occur in relation to surrounding streets is relevant to the urban design plan; so are the linkages between a city convention centre and the hotels and restaurants around it, or the new activities that can re-connect a city to its waterfront as riverside industry declines.

The urban design implications of all aspects of the plan must be spelled out. Will the intended configuration of streets permit or impede views of the bay? Will bulk and height restrictions maintain visual corridors to the capitol tower? What type of urban tissue will the regulations produce? What are the functional problems or aesthetic opportunities of areas where urban systems collide? The visual results of intended decisions should be depicted, for example, the view of the expressway at the foot of the colonial alley, or the scale jump between the historic shopping street and the high-rise office buildings that will rise behind it.

The recommendations of the urban design plan should will not rise above the level of good intentions unless they are related to means of implementation,therefore the plan be prescriptive as well as advisory. As part of an adopted urban plan, the prescriptions have legal power and can be translated into the city's implementation programme. Prescriptions will, in general, be contained in the two-dimensional land use plan, the zoning code and the provisions of any other legal controls. The rest must be achieved through advice and suasion.

Important as the plan is, it will change; yet when it changes the public realm will still be there. The design of the public realm should provide a strong beginning for whatever the future will bring and should leave the options open for events and conditions that cannot be predicted.

Public taste and the public realm
Each city has its own traditions, symbols, contexts and preferences from which the architecture of its public realm should be derived. Although urban populations are multicultural and have varied tastes,[8] the public realm can, I believe, be designed to appeal across the span of taste cultures, because people have more widely shared expectations for public architecture than they have for their own houses, or perhaps because they do not expect to exert their private tastes over the public realm to the extent they do over their own houses.[9]

How should public tastes and preferences be elicited? How tightly should the design of the public realm be tied to prevailing tastes? What should be the role of artistic innovation in the design of the public realm, if artistic innovation, by definition, outrages present tastes? Who should decide the answers to these questions?

To what extent and at what level the design of the public realm should meet present tastes; whether it should suit the present tastes of only some groups; or future tastes; or the individual preferences of designers; should be argued out (preferably with public participation) during the design process. The consensus arrived at should be reflected in the design guidelines and recommendations and in the selection of architects for public projects.

Norms for the public realm
Although the public realm must meet the needs of the individual city, some prescriptions seem to be constant even as the options multiply. The public realm should evolve from its context. It should be tough and durable to accommodate the intense use it will receive over the years. It should relate in a complex way to the private uses, structures and people it serves and should be scaled to these at all levels, from the private doorstep to the regional freeway network.

The realm should include both the civic and the public. It should be a system-wide network but, even were money no object, it should not be so vast or so overbearing as to make government seem oppressive. Yet it should be generous and abundant in order to help citizens and visitors feel welcome and well served in the city.

The public realm's design should be more general than the set of functions that it must support at any one time; it is a basket to dip hands into, rather than a glove that fits snugly. A public realm that satisfies civic criteria for toughness and abundance will have a degree of ability to withstand unforeseen change.

Some prescriptions for the writing and drawing of design guidelines
A primary purpose of design guidelines is to share information on the city's aims for an area with those who intend to design and build in it, so that decisions at different design scales can be made in cognizance of the intentions of others. To help inform private-sector designers, the public urban designer may undertake a 'learning from' study,[10] analysing the symbols of the city and the architectural character of buildings and spaces, describing traditional relationships between urban form and topography or buildings and streets, showing how these have changed over the years and suggesting new and historic exemplars that may be pleasing to citizens or useful for new development. Demonstrating urban design aims by discussing what is good or bad in the existing city may clarify the guidelines and make them

understandable.

Heights, proportions, scales, scale juxtapositions, materials, colours, relations between new and existing – all these are areas for description, discussion and prescription in the guidelines. The degree of control established by the guidelines will vary with the type of neighbourhood or street, but should be the least possible. Design guidelines must be complex and tuned to the layered realities of the areas they guide. For example, if one street consists of historic buildings, new structures and honky-tonk, it may require three different but parallel sets of guidelines. Civic buildings, public buildings and private buildings also require different and parallel guidelines, as do the various building types of the private sector. Criteria evolved for a 50-storey office complex should not be applied to a 5-storey art museum. Because urban sites are constrained, the urban designer can often predict the approach private building designers are likely to take to particular sites and can set the guidelines in terms of the probable plans, and even some of the details, of future private projects.

Because guidelines are intended to establish an *a priori* rapport between the individual designer and the city, they should be evocative rather than prescriptive and should open opportunity and induce enthusiasm rather than constrict and smother. Guidelines should suggest by nuance not mandate by fiat. They should convey mental images through words and drawings. The painting of word pictures requires allusive, poetic writing. Drawings should not look like architectural drawings; they should be sketchier, freer, able to be filled out by the imagination of others. Nevertheless, urban design drawings should distinguish clearly between a stated intention, a predicted reaction to a city-initiated intervention and a vision. In addition to depicting the desired general character of an area, guidelines must show what the city provides or requires and must suggest the likely private sector reaction to what is provided or required. The need to show both action and reaction implies a level of kineticism in urban design mapping and sketching and demands the ability to describe predicted reactions without designing specific, individual buildings – no mean feat.

Guidelines need to be tested through the design of individual buildings and should be reformulated, where necessary, as a result of the tests. The agency that promulgates the guidelines should set itself the exercise of trying to do the worst designs that would be possible within its own guidelines. The results can be both sobering and liberating.

Design review
The courts have ruled that beauty is an urban amenity subject to theprotection of the policepower, and that it may bepromulgation of regulatory mesures and the review of discretionary boards. However, the judges have omitted to discuss the standards by which beauty may be defined or the processes through which it may be equitably deemed to be present. Local authorities have reacted by appointing 'experts' (usually local architects) who use their own discretion in assigning beauty or lack of it to the works of others. The limits set on capriciousness, authoritarianism, or venality in such a system are those internal to the individual review board members. This is rule by man rather than rule by law.

In proceedings based solely on taste, the supplicant architect is left perplexed and time and money are lost in frustrating attempts, by scheming rather than designing, to anticipate or to follow the dicta of 'experts' whose tastes and philosophies differ from the architect's own or are so capricious as to be incomprehensible.

Aesthetically, too, the aim is not achieved. Any artist could have told the lawmakers that you cannot legislate beauty and that attempts to do so by the use of experts will result not only in gross injustice but in an ugly deadness in the environment.

Beauty escapes in the pursuit of safety, which promotes a simplistic sameness over a varied vitality. It withers under the edicts of today's aging architectural revolutionaries who man the review boards and who have achieved aesthetic certainty.

In sum, design review is a lawyer's, not an artist's, solution to the problem of obtaining quality in the public realm. This criticism of the design review process, first published in 1972 [11], has become more not less relevant with time. Design review turns architectural designers into legal strategists, it suppresses artistry and innovation and, like other forms of absolute power, it corrupts those who wield it and the processes they preside over. However there seems little likelihood that design review as a method of achieving public aesthetic aims will be abandoned – in fact, the trend is in the other direction. Therefore sophisticated public agencies should devise methods of protecting against its depredations.

Where design review is mandated, the following safeguards should be instituted to help establish due process and maintain equity:

Quantitative controls should substitute for discretionary controls wherever possible. The use of a design review board with discretionary powers should be limited as far as possible and should follow after the exercise of staff review.

The design review board should be a broadly mixed group that includes agency members, design professionals, community representatives, business representatives and a lawyer or two. Equity and busy schedules would be well served if the board were to consist of members and alternates.

Where judgement and discretion are required, these should be based on explicit design criteria, promulgated through written and illustrated design guidelines that are available to the public, to architects and to intending developers. The design review board should be well instructed on the requirements of due process in their review. The designers among them should not be permitted to act as architects. Board members should be required to produce written opinions explaining why a project does or does not meet the criteria.

All design review requirements should be consolidated into one process. Projects should not be subject to double jeopardy at the hands of disagreeing agencies.

Not all projects should be reviewed; only those whose location or nature makes them affected with the public interest.

All meetings of the design review board should be sunshine meetings.

The time spent by the design review board on a project should be long enough to ensure that the full implications, particularly the economic and functional implications, of the board's aesthetic recommendations are understood by the board.

A time limit should be set for the response of the board to a design proposal; design review staff and board members should be made aware of the narrow time limits most projects must work within, during design.

There should be a means of appeal available from the board's dicta. This appeal should be to a committee that has a broad understanding of city aims and objectives. Time limits for the response of the appeal board should be brief.

Although design requirements for different aspects of the city may be different, the blanket of design review should fall, as much as possible, equitably across the whole city. The spelling out of design criteria should help to avoid inequitable or venal applications of design review.

The role of architects in urban design
The foregoing has shown that there are many possible roles for

architects in the city. On one level, the smallest building or part of a building can be designed urbanistically, where this means setting it in lively discourse with its context, designing with due regard to its purpose and importance in the urban hierarchy, understanding the relation of its own public and private spaces to the spaces of the public realm and meeting urban requirements for access, bulk, height, safety and light.

Crane's 'Capital Web' suggests one way of conceptualising the role and control span of the urban designer whose client is the city. The community activist, who represents a section of the community, will have a different scope and focus in area and subject matter, a different process for performing tasks and communicating with client and public and a different product. The architect of an individual building will have another and the urban visionary and publicist yet another. In each role the designer is restricted by the client's location within the urban polity and by the scope of the client's responsibility for implementation. This is ill-defined territory in both architecture and urban design.

Whatever the role, the architect needs not only a knowledge of the particular building type or area and an understanding of its context, but also what constitutes appropriate behaviour for that role and where, in the role, design control ends and design suasion begins. Architects' belief that they can control more than their client controls may be a prime factor in the failure of architects' recommendations for the city.

The present confusion

Lack of clarity in defining and allocating roles in the overlapping design tasks of the city leads to confusion. The architect of a civic building may find frustration in having to satisfy urban design guidelines evolved for the design of office buildings by urban designers who forgot to allow for civic buildings in their thinking. Or the urban designer trying to devise sidewalk improvements to suit a new transit mall may run foul of the city agencies that provide street lights. Or the architect of a museum may try with little success to persuade the landscape architect of the park opposite to design it to go with the museum's entrances and open space needs. On the design review committee the hapless architect may discover, not an urban design statesman, but an architect *manque*, who disagrees with the cladding material chosen and specifies a personal preference by the name of the product and the manufacturer. Or design guidelines may require that all streets be lined with trees, regardless of whether they block the view of store fronts, street signs or historic facades; or that 25 percent of the project's open space be in grass, regardless of location, shape or function – thereby removing from consideration many of the world's most loved piazzas. Entire building plans may be dictated to private architects by public sector designers, without concern for requirements from the inside out and with only limited understanding of requirements from the outside in.

In short, designers at many levels, backed by their own clients, may feel they have rights in an individual project or urban area. Such tangles occur because architects in both the public and the private sector have little idea of the nature and limits of their role or of due process (or indeed of fair play) in the on-going business of urban design for the city. The adjudication of territories and negotiation of areas of control in the above scenarios (all of which are from real life) should be based on the rule of law, and government, as the mandated planner for the whole, should sponsor the finding of equitable arbitration procedures. Government instead appoints design review boards, showing itself thereby to be ignorant of the issue and unwilling to re-think the problem. In any case, avoiding unjust coersion and aesthetic enervation on the hand and aesthetic libertinage on the other,

would require of the drafter of aesthetic regulations, the wisdom of Solomon.

A further reason for the present confusion is that during the 1960s there was a wholesale turning away by urban planners from physical design toward social and economic planning. This entirely worthy re-appraisal of the role of the planner had the effect of keeping major planning talent away from traditional planning tasks and eventually from the under-funded public agencies. Their place was frequently taken by architects and young lawyers (for the implementation tasks of planning). In the schools, with most planners training as economic and social activists, urban design moved its province into architecture, instead of maintaining a straddling balance between architecture and planning.

The result is that those who practice urban design for the public sector today are often lawyers without planning training, or architects who may or may not have some urban design training from an architecture school. Such urban designers lack the basic knowledge or urban economics and politics that would introduce both reality and room for negotiating into their plans. However, their training in architecture is often inadequate too, as they became urbanists before they gained experience in the design and construction of buildings. Lacking urban knowledge and architectural depth, urban designers fall between two stools; planners declare their prescriptions unrealistic and architects find their designs untalented. In addition, the field of urban design, lodged as it is in other academic departments, has been slow to form a separate discipline backed by scholarship and research. Urban designers, therefore, have little theory upon which to base their opinions. They borrow theoretical hand-me-downs from architecture – the most recent from Post-Modernism, before that from the Athens Charter. They also borrow models from the European city. In any case, the ethos of the American city, with its strengths and its weaknesses, is seldom the basis for the promulgating of public sector urban design recommendations.

Over the last 30 years most architects have come to agree that the design of the city cannot be produced by one architect or even by one team. But in the formulation of aesthetic controls, cities often promote the vision of one urban design team. This lack of sophistication in urban design could be acceptable if urban design were a small sub-section in the planning agency and urban planning were able to focus its main tasks on the social and economic needs of the city; but, in the general turning away from social and economic concerns, what has been left to agency planners is traditional physical planning and urban design. Now that we have architects and lawyers practicing planning, major emphasis is placed in planning agencies on urban design and on legal mechanisms for controlling design – and on the most simple-minded of those mechanisms, aesthetic zoning and design review.

In some cities, design control is used to paper over other troubles. If a community reacts against proposals to increase the density of a neighbourhood the city may nevertheless bow to economic pressures and permit the increase, then try to assuage public anger through the offer of design control on the offending project or projects, to be applied through the city's urban design department. The fight that then ensues between developers' architects, who are highly experienced in the building type but uninformed on local urban needs and agency designers, who are probably underpaid and unsophisticated in both planning and architecture, is another recipe for disaster.

Conclusion

The pulsating masses of 'no's' that emerge from today's urban design regulations may seem a far cry from the early visions of the *Ville Radieuse;* but perhaps they are not. Both are the result of architects' aiming to control more than they should, though in fairness to Le Corbusier it should be noted that in these designs he was acting as a polemicist.

Admitting into urban design the untidy reality of urban decision-making is a risky procedure that designers try to avoid, because all designers experience loss of design control as the sensation of drowning. Yet the infringements of reality on the independence of the individual designer may act as a goad to imagination and creativity, leading to better designs. In this essay I have trodden the terrain of several professions making sweeps over a wide plain, I have tried to bring some urban ideas and issues into focus. By describing the spectra of public and private, surveying strategies for implementation, and discussing the multiple roles of architects and urban designers in the city, I

have hoped to come up with a rich definition of the problems of architectural urbanism. At the end, I have left urban design in a state of confusion without proposals for how to get us out. I feel we have had a plethora of over-simple nostrums. The immediate task should be to define the complexity and consider what the real issues are. But I have included guidelines for finding the solution, and guidelines for writing the guidelines.

Urban design requires thoughtful, knowledgeable and able designers, who can intervene in the urban processes in a supportive and understanding way and who will know when, in their given role, it is appropriate to design, and when it is more creative *not* to.

This is an expanded version of a paper presented for a symposium, 'The public realm: Architecture and Society', at the College of Architecture of the University of Kentucky, 1985.

Notes

1 Mark Lilla, 'The Great Museum Muddle', The New Republic, 8 April 1985, pp 25-30.
2 John Kenneth Galbraith, The Affluent Society, Houghton Mifflin Company, Boston, Mass, 1958.
3 David A Crane, 'The City Symbolic', The Journal of the American Institute of Planners, November 1960, pp 280-292; and 'Chandigarh Reconsidered: The Dynamic City', *Journal of the American Institute of Architects,* May 1960, pp 32-9.
4 My analysis of the qualities of monumental architecture owes a great deal to my discussions on this subject with Robert Venturi, since the early 1960s.
5 Galen Cranz, *The Politics of Park Design: A History of Urban Parks in America,* The MIT Press, Cambridge, Mass, 1982.

6 William H Whyte, *The Social Life of Small Urban Spaces,* The Conservation Foundation, Washington, DC, 1980.
7 Articles on San Francisco zoning: Gerald D Adams, 'A Last Ditch Effort to Save Downtown San Francisco', pp 4-11; and George A Williams, 'Fine Points of the San Francisco Plan', in *Planning,* February 1984, pp 12-5.
8 Herbert J Gans, *Popular Culture and High Culture: An Analysis and Evaluation of Taste,* Basic Books Inc, New York, 1974.
9 Denise Scott Brown, 'Architectural Taste in a Pluralistic Society', *The Harvard Architectural Review,* Spring 1980, pp 41-51.
10 Robert Venturi, Denise Scott Brown, Steven Izenour, *Learning from Las Vegas,* revised edition, The MIT Press, Cambridge, Mass, 1977.
11 *ibid,* pp 164-5.

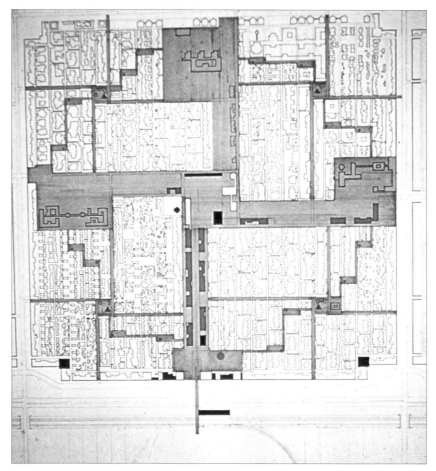

CAPITAL WET PLAN 1959, NEW CITY CHANDIGARH STUDIO

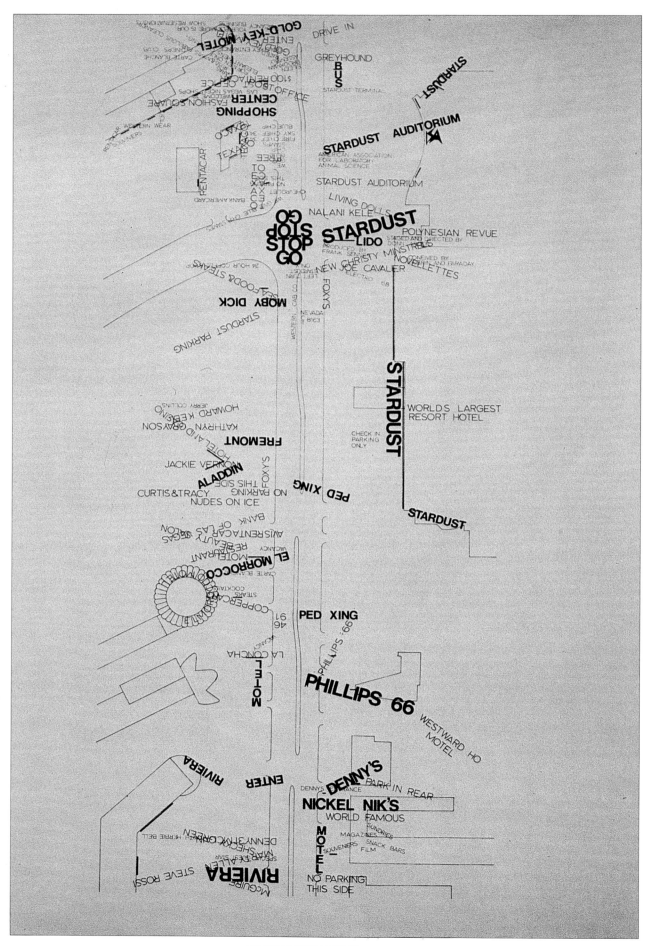

LAS VEGAS. STRIP MESSAGE ANALYSIS

THE RISE AND FALL OF COMMUNITY ARCHITECTURE

SKETCH FOR IMPROVEMENT OF SOUTH STREET, PHILADELPHIA

This article is an edited version of a lecture given at the Tate Gallery Symposium, The Rise and Fall of Community Architecture, organised by The Academy Group. Denise Scott Brown's lecture was followed by a discussion chaired by Robert Thorne, involving a number of invited participants including Martin Pawley and Simon Jenkins, and concluding with contributions from the audience.

Community architecture is the most recent expression of ideas and ideals that have, in one form or another, accompanied the modern development of the profession. The history of social concern in architecture predates the Modern Movement. Arts and Crafts architects and designers, for example, saw socialism as central to their artistic philosophy. But it was the Modern Movement that defined the social tasks of architecture for our century, placing the social component in uneasy competition with the aesthetic and translating the urge to do good into a focus on housing, with particular stress on social housing. Social concern, we are told, did not cross the Atlantic with the Modern movement, thanks to Henry Russell Hitchcock and Philip Johnson who ignored this aspect of the new architecture when they introduced it to America in 1932 through their book, The International Style. This is half the truth. The planner, Catherine Bauer, made an exhaustive survey of housing in Europe and, in 1934, published Modern Housing. This excellent book did introduce Modern architectural social philosophy to America, but architects didn't read it. Actually, I suspect that socially concerned architects in America did read it; the problem was, and is, that if you become interested in social housing in America you soon realise housing the poor isn't primarily a design, or even a technical, problem; it is first an economic and political problem. Therefore architects who become involved in housing have, since the New Deal, stopped being architects and turned

economists and administrators.

In England, World War II and its aftermath brought stark austerity and a great rebuilding task. During the late 1940s and early 1950s there were two architectural reactions to the war: a turning away from austerity, which resulted in the frou-frou architecture of the Festival of Britain, and a burst of social idealism particularly among students. The ex-service students, who exerted an enormous influence on English architecture schools in the early 1950s, saw social housing as their first concern. When I entered the AA as a fourth-year student in 1952, I found there an invigorating air of high endeavour and a major focus on social concern. At that time the Smithsons were part of the Independent Group at the Institute of Contemporary Art. Some AA students sought out this exciting couple, who were not then teaching at the AA; before they became gurus to the profession, the Smithsons became architectural comrades-in-arms to a small band of AA rebels.

As a child in Africa, I was continually aware of the differences between what I saw around me and what I read in books. Our books in the 1940s came largely from England. Those in Africa who applied English norms to the African visual environment pointed out strong schisms between what was and what they felt should be. The same difference between 'is' and 'ought' fascinated the New Brutalists who rediscovered what early Modern architects had discovered before them – the beauties of the ugly

31

architecture of industrial areas. But in the milieu of the Independent Group, Brutalist interest spread beyond factories to commercial architecture, popular culture and more basically, to how people really live, as opposed to how architects, planners or society say they ought to live. As I understood the Smithson phrase 'active socioplastics', it meant that architects should design for the real life of the street and for the way communities actually work, even if the results are not conventionally pleasing. There was, I think, an unspoken desire to derive, from a community life that is not immediately beautiful, a deeper beauty, and an intention not to abandon architecture but to make it socially relevant. Also, there was the obstinate hope that socially responsible architecture could be beautiful, even if the beauty was an agonised one. This is, in a way, a functionalist approach. It says 'Look around you with eyes which see'. (Le Corbusier talked of 'eyes which do not see'.) 'Look at grain elevators, smoke stacks, the tops of ships, street architecture, commercial architecture and popular art, and learn from these. If you do, you will become more useful to your society, yet freshen your aesthetic eye and be a better artist as well.' That's maybe a romantic notion but I still hold to it. The Smithsons dropped socioplastics. They said sociology had to develop before architecture could use it. I disagree. My theory is that urban sociologists will never know about things physical. They have hang-ups about art. They think it is elitist. So architects will have to learn sociology, not the other way round. We at least get a verbal education in school. They don't get a visual one. If there's going to be any meeting of the disciplines, it will have to be achieved by us.

In Philadelphia, in 1958, I discovered that the vision of the future proposed for many American cities was the CIAM vision that the Smithsons had found too rigid. Urban renewal American-style called for demolition of vast areas of 'blight' and their rebuilding in approximations of Le Corbusier's *Ville Radieuse*. Downtown was to be encircled by a ring of expressways to bring people from the suburbs to the high-rise towers at the centre. However, by 1958, criticism of this form of renewal was starting in America. My professors at Penn complained that American re-development projects might look like European social housing, but housed the rich not the poor. This was because the urban renewal programme, although it had its origins in New Deal policies sponsored by Roosevelt to help America through the Depression, was drafted to benefit many interests in the city, in order to get their support. This meant that the programme did not, in the end, house the poor. I think you will find in England, too, that people in council housing were not the poorest of the population, they were those Shaw called the deserving poor. But in America, re-development housing was for the upper-middle classes.

At the same time Levittown was being built. This was social housing the American way. In America, government induced the private sector, through economic measures, to build the equivalent of English council housing. Although technological innovation was involved, merchant builders such as Levitt and Sons, who built the Levittowns, realised that only 30 per cent of the cost of a suburban house lies in construction, therefore advanced construction technology could save on only 30 per cent of the price. In the technology of organization of the building industry lay the real opportunity for saving. The Levitts integrated the building industry vertically, becoming their own suppliers and warehouser. This meant they could design products to their own specification and more important, control delivery dates and streamline on-site construction processes. This aspect of construction technology should be better understood by architects who hope to solve housing problems through industrialised housing.

Herbert Gans, who was my professor of urban sociology in my first semester at Penn, moved to Levittown in that same year, to observe how the new community organised itself. Earlier he had studied poor families in the west end of Boston as they were being removed through urban renewal. In the late 1940s and early 1950s Michael Young and Peter Wilmott studied the London poor to learn what happened to people who were moved away from their homes and families to the new towns. I think Gans was influenced by their work.

So I went from the New Brutalists to Gans. What they shared was the idea I had found intriguing as a cultural colonial in Africa: that you should look as open-mindedly as you could at real patterns and try to build from them – for both moral and aesthetic reasons. The Smithsons' belief that physical form should mirror rather than direct social organization was expressed in their Greenlanes housing project, which greatly interested us at the time. Ironically, streets in the air caused their own social problems; you need streets on the ground to generate the multiple and intense activities that bring safety. But these were important ideas in the development of architecture and the philosophy and approach that underlay them was correct.

While teaching at Penn, I spent my spare moments photographing in Philadelphia, adding to a collection of pop photography Robert Scott Brown and I started in Europe. I learned to analyse the words in ads; some are wonderful. For example, 'O.R. Lumpkin auto refinishing. Wrecks our specialty. We take the dent out of accident'. Someone should write a dissertation on billboard words. At the edge of town I found another pop urban environment scorned and hated by architects, the commercial strip. I set out to discover how to take good photographs of it.

In my course work in the social sciences at Penn, I began to understand that things don't happen in cities by whim or by architectural fiat, but that urban order derives, at least in part, from the fact that many people in cities make similar decisons.

15ᵀᴴ

From these decisions, and in relation to topograhy and geometry, patterns evolve. Urban designers had better understand these patterns. They were first documented in the 19th and 20th centuries by European economists – Von Thunen, Christaller, Loesch and Weber – and later expanded by American economists and regional scientists – Haig, Hoyt, Isard, Perloff, Harris, Lowry, Alonso and others. Their analyses started with documenting how crops were cultivated in concentric circles in relation to markets and ended with complex computer studies of urban regions. The geometric patterns that emerge from the analyses are curiously evocative. The cusps in the tent diagrams of urban rent theory look like the skylines of cities. From the air, the towns of the American plains seem to form the hierarchic patterns documented by Christaller in relation to market journeys. 'Social physics', translated on to the land, has always been fascinating to me. I feel urban architects, if they are to be successful, must realise that land settlement is, at least in part, an orderly system, to be understood. They should see the patterns that derive from social and economic forces as part of their muse, part of their inspiration and should, where possible, use rather than negate these patterns. Architects must at times work against the patterns. For example, site a university on Main street and, if there is demand for land, the pattern of shops, offices and housing will distort but re-form around this foreign body in the system.

You must understand urban economics if you are an urban designer and you must understand it particularly well if you intend to work against economic pressures, because strength and power are required to do so. Nevertheless you can't work against all the forces all the time and why would you do so if you didn't have to, if you could use the pressures to take you where you want to go? This idea was an important addendum to my thinking – that one should not merely understand the way a society operates but should try to work with its forces, to the extent that one can without too far compromising goals. I think it's called American pragmatism. It is also an effort to develop a green thumb for cities.

During this time some aspects of the social critique of American planning heard at Penn and Berkeley were introduced to a wider circle by the writer Jane Jacobs. There was mounting public criticism that urban renewal, as then practiced, did not achieve social aims, that it looked ugly, that its architecture was dead and that the public voted with their feet by not using the places architects designed. This criticism was made part of the exegesis of the New Left. In 1962, James Baldwin published an article on poverty in the *New Yorker*. In it, page after page of diatribe against American society sat surrounded by *New Yorker*-style advertisements for luxuries and the good life. The article went like wild-fire through our planning school. As the New Left developed, social scientists became social activists; students

chose projects in low-income, inner-city areas that we used to call 'the ghetto'. We stopped saying 'negro' and started saying 'black', because black leaders told us we should, pushing blacks and whites to accept that 'black is beautiful'.

The theoretical underpinnings for social planning were provided by social thinkers such as Gans, Webber, Davidoff and Reiner who taught that important planning decisions should be made by people not by planners. They warned that planners and architects had upper middle-class values and asked that they respect other people's views too. How do you find out about people's values? Gans said that people elect politicians who represent their values, therefore planners must heed what politicians say. Planning, Gans felt, should be part of politics. Social activists such as Davidoff and Reiner pointed out that the poor, and particularly the black poor, were unrepresented or under-represented politically in the 1960s. Planners, they felt, should become advocates for those unrepresented people, as lawyers are advocates for their clients.

So the 'advocacy planning' movement was born. It was a creature of the New Left and it appealed particularly to students but its influence changed procedures in planning agencies, giving greater power to local communities to plan for themselves. Eventually 'advocacy architecture' followed and, with help from the AIA, architecture workshops were set up in many communities to give free architectural help to low-income groups. In 1961 Planners for Equal Opportunity, a social planning group, was formed. Ten years later they held a meeting in Washington at which a couple of British journalists were present. They returned and reported the proceedings in England. Since then the English have led the world in community planning. If you think I am being sarcastic, I am!

In 1963 I made a survey of a group called the Neighbourhood Garden Association who were working in low-income areas, helping people fix up vacant lots and turn them into flower gardens. It was a strange group that puzzled and outraged the social planners, who saw upper-class ladies from the suburbs working with the black matriarchy and succeeding better than the planners did. Yet they did so because both groups believed that flowers were good for people and would given them good character and that reading Bible stories to children was good for their souls. The upper middle-class professionals did not share, and were indeed horrified by, this value system but it seemed to work. My job was to show how it worked.

In 1965 I moved to California. I once read in an English architectural journal that 'It was Cedric Price who first discovered Los Angeles. He discovered it in 1961.' That architectural jingoism angers both the African and the American in me. If you want to be flippant, it was Esther McCoy who first discovered Los Angeles and she discovered it in 1932. In fact the School of City Planning at Penn taught that architects and urbanists can't

JUNIPER

13TH

D

afford to scorn or ignore the urbanism of Los Angeles. It's not chaos but a new order that's emerging; we should try to understand it.

Learning from Las Vegas

It was in this spirit that I first visited Las Vegas in 1965. Unlike the dead spaces of architect-designed urban renewal, the Las Vegas Strip was somewhere that people actually went. They seemed to enjoy it. I didn't see frowns on their faces as if they were being coerced into going there. They voted with their feet for what they liked. Hate it though you may, people use it and like it. They don't live on the Strip. They go there to spend an evening or a few days. Critics who say 'You wouldn't want to live there yourself' are distorting the Las Vegas reality. Las Vegans don't live on the Strip. They are proud of their residential and recreational areas, set well away from the Strip. The Las Vegas environments gave me a shiver. Was it hate or love? I couldn't tell, but it was profoundly jolting. The jolt gets you out of an aesthetic rut. That is why I felt Bob and I could learn from it and invited him to visit it with me in 1966.

In 1968 we started analysing the Strip, with our students we

relevant; hoping through study of the 'messy vitality' of Las Vegas to learn how to design in a way that would not cause social harm through applying unnecessarily rigid aesthetic criteria. Yet, in the end, the main answer to the question 'Well, what *did* you learn from Las Vegas?' is that we learned to reassess the role of symbolism in architecture and that this helped guide our search for an appropriate architecture for a 'Post-Modern' period. That our ideas led to a new formal order as rigid as the Modern and to a set of architectural preoccupations far from the social and aesthetic concerns that drove us was not what we intended and has more to do with the nature of our profession than with us. As Venturi said 'Plus ca change'.

South Street, Philadelphia

While we were analysing Las Vegas, we were also prescribing for South Street in Philadelphia. This was an old commercial strip threatened by an expressway. It was a long street that stretched between Philadelphia's two rivers. It had seen every immigrant group come up it. Along its length communities were subtended like beads on a string. There were Irish in the west, blacks in the east, Italians and Jews in the middle. Precursors of

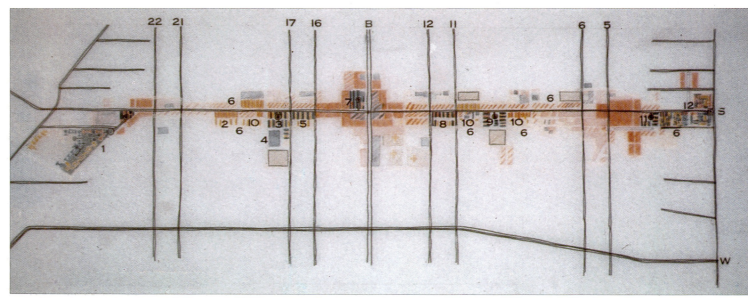

ACTIVITIES MAP, SOUTH STREET, PHILADELPHIA

took cross-cuts through it to see what kind of space it was. We tried to relate Strip space to traditional spaces that we all knew such as the Eastern bazaar, the Medieval street and the landscape of Versailles. We began to see that urban space does not need to be defined as it has been historically, by walls, it can be defined in other ways. The Strip is defined by movement and by the signs that communicate with you as you drive down it at 30 miles an hour – great signs that you can see from the air before you land. Symbol in space before form in space; that is the order in this landscape. We also analysed the words of the signs and the juxtapositions of symbols or of signs and architecture. On one level the combinations are violent but on another they form a new whole, related to the automobile, to a mass society, if you like, and to mass use – although a good eye is kept on individuals as well. The whole mixed media environment tells you something of the orgy you will have if you come to Las Vegas. People go to Las Vegas feeling (to quote Alan Lapidus) 'afraid something wonderful might happen'.

Of course our study was of much more than signs and people who consider Las Vegas at night only don't understand what we were after. We were trying, *inter alia*, to make ourselves socially

the yuppies were approaching from both ends and the centre. It was a thriving shopping street in the 1920s, a market for residents around it and famous for its jazz clubs. When people started to leave for the suburbs, it lost its 'carriage trade' and began to decline. By the time our work started the expressway had been threatened for ten years. Lacking expectations, South Street had grown seedy. Neither its economic methods nor its architecture had changed in twenty years and on it lived some of the poorest people of Philadelphia. The social planner who invited me to join the planning team said that although she didn't believe in architecture and thought that we should be tackling the social and economic problems of cities first, people were going to be pushed out of their houses onto the streets before we could ever deal with jobs or education. She added 'If you can like Las Vegas, we trust you not to neaten up South Street at the expense of its people.'

The expressway threatened 6,000 mainly poor people for whom there was no public housing. The social planners felt the community needed to present its own plan and image for what South Street could be without an expressway. Would we become advocate planners and architects for this community? We had to go before the community board to see if we would be acceptable as volunteer workers and advocates for them. One of the reasons they accepted us was that we had a concern in common. Bob Venturi, apart from being an architect, was a fruit merchant. He had inherited his father's business on South Street so we were all threatened by the expressway. He (and later, he and I) supervised the running of the business, which supported the architect, until finally the roles reversed and the architect was supporting the fruit merchant. Then we went out of business. If you know the terms 'succession' and 'invasion' you will understand that the Italian and Jewish merchants on South Street were slowly moving out. Some of the new merchants were black, but most were young intellectuals running art galleries and 'collectables' shops.

South Street was our first 'Main Street' project and the first community project we undertook as practitioners not academics. We set about studying its many facets. We learned that South Street retailers could never again depend solely on a local market for their goods and services and that, to save an old main street in a low-income city area, it is necessary to find new uses for its buildings, based on their location and the quality of their

suggested, should be to erect a banner over the street, paint one sign and rehabilitate one building, to show someone cares. This would be a quick beginning.

Our land-use maps for South Street looked quite unclear because we gave separate attention to individual sites and to different floor levels. We didn't show the whole block in the colour of its dominant use. If you try to represent land use in all its complexity in low-income, inner-city communities, your land use plan looks like a bruise, with small patches of blue and yellow, red and purple. Our transportation proposal argued that in the rich areas of Philadelphia planners would not dream of replacing existing roads with an expressway. Instead they recommend coupled one-way streets. Do the same thing here, we said, make South and Bainbridge Streets a one-way couple and Washington Street an on-grade arterial. Make a plaid out of the Philadelphia street grid. In that way, all streets will be used to best advantage and we won't need an expressway.

As a planner I had been taught that land use and transportation are 'inextricably intertwingled' as Robert Mitchell, my professor at Penn, used to put it. So I was surprised when I learned the community did not wish my transportation plan to be shown.

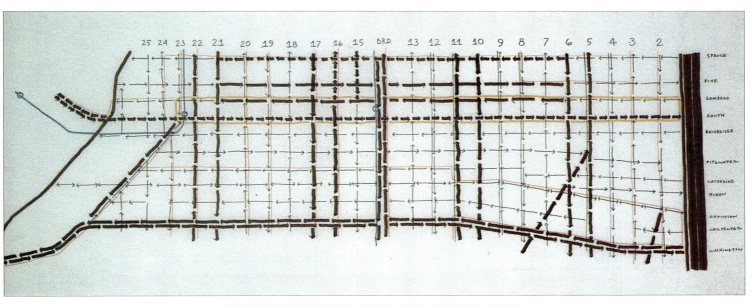

CROSSTOWN CORRIDOR TRAFFIC PATTERN, SOUTH STREET, PHILADELPHIA

architecture. These uses should attract people to the area but should not induce revolutionary change that will displace residents and demolish neighbourhoods. We discovered that South Street already had a series of overlapping markets, drawing people for a variety of purposes from New Jersey and the outskirts of Philadelphia as well as from the central city. We found that effective planning for old inner-city communities involves regional economics, local economics, architecture, historic preservation, knowledge of transportation and construction, understanding of urban community structure, dynamics and familiarity with methods for achieving democratic consensus.

We worked for the 'Crosstown Community' as architects and planners for four years. Our plan recommended starting renewal of the Crosstown community by introducing one-stop shopping for social services for low-income people in two existing buildings, one on either side of Broad Street. Community renewal started through public investment at these sites would generate private renewal nearby, but on a small scale to suit the needs of those immediately around it. This meant local community members could get in first and establish a hold in certain areas before larger scale renewal overtook the street. The very first act, we

They felt its provisions would set other communities against them, making them vulnerable to manipulation between communities by the Department of Transportation. The community vetoed one other scheme: some architects recommended getting donations of paint and painting all the side walls of houses where buildings had been demolished on the street. The community said 'If we had enough people with the ability to organise doing that, why would we waste their time on something so futile? We need them for other things such as banging on the mayor's door'. They also believed we should not waste community time on, for example, land use surveys because political activities were more important. So I began to learn interesting and important lessons in planning from the members of this low-income, black community – helped by their brilliant leader Alice Lipscomb and their brilliant and merry lawyer, Robert Sugarman.

The social planners liked our plans. They were glad that we hadn't designed buildings because it was too early to do so. They approved of our designating by number the kinds of buildings and types of programmes that should be sponsored in different locations. On our maps government actions were depicted in one way and the type of reaction that might be expected from the private sector, in another. This followed Robert Mitchell's dictum that planners should be careful to distinguish between what they recommend and what they expect will happen. It is also important to differentiate between intentions, projections, predictions and predelictions. Architects should understand these differences too.

East Poplar, Philadelphia

Our next community project was for East Poplar in Philadelphia. This was a Ukranian neighbourhood for which an early urban renewal plan was made in 1948. It was a 'state of the art' plan at the time, full of good hope. It expressed high aspirations for a 'balanced community' but it ended in a law suit when blacks moved into East Poplar and the redevelopment authority changed the plan, erecting low-income housing but not the middle or moderate income housing that would make for a balanced community. A black city planning student, Maurice Shannon, sued the redevelopment authority for abrogating the plan and won. As part of the settlement we were hired as court appointed planners and architects to help decide what redress the community should have. I found myself in the middle, in a conflict between middle-class blacks who wanted the plan as originally proposed and low-income black matriarchs who wanted their subsidised housing. I found I could get along very well with the matriarchy; perhaps we recognised a common link. In the end it was decided that more housing of different kinds would be built; we recommended that the city should also sponsor a project area committee where community people could be represented in planning for the area. Thanks to the civil rights movement and the social planners, Philadelphia communities could at that time do their own planning through their own elected representatives and their own paid staff planners. In setting up a democratic participatory process we recommended that the project area committee represent all neighbourhood interests and also all groups who could exercise a veto vote, be they low-income people, storekeepers, artists or others. There should be two kinds of democracy at work, a direct democracy of public meetings, where a vote is taken, and a representational democracy of the project area committee that gave the planners direction. I also invited people to write me letters to tell me what they wanted, and many of them did.

Jim Thorpe, Pennsylvania

Jim Thorpe is the little town in Pennsylvania where coal was first discovered. Its old town consists basically of one main street that slopes up a river valley between steep, wooded mountains. It was once one of the richest towns in the United States. With the coal barons came sumptuous mansions and proud street architecture; on West Broadway, the town's main street, it was as if Philadelphia's Broad Street had been wedged between two mountains. The street was lined by a hierarchy of monumental public buildings, the station, county hall, the navigation building, the library, the opera house – even a jail. They seemed meant for a larger city.

We carefully analysed the old town, building by building, following in spirit Patrick Geddes' analyses of Indian villages. We also studied the economy of the surrounding region which was becoming a white water rafting, canoeing and skiing area. We investigated other competing and complementary resort areas. We recommended that the historical link between Jim Thorpe and its river and canal be re-established. Then we suggested ways in which the townspeople could use their heritage of river, canal, rail, and buildings to attract some of the growing tourist trade but not so much that it would overwhelm them. Design guidelines for the area were all on a quite small scale involving mainly painting and fixing up. We proposed one

street re-routing and the addition of a parking structure and made suggestions for rebuilding a vacant lot. They are still using this plan years later.

Princeton

At Princeton the problem was to maintain the character and image of a small university town when it was being overrun by yuppies and the elderly rich. I am not showing you the plan but another aspect of participatory planning: the offering of alternatives. The social planners warned us not to say to people 'I am the expert, here is your plan' but instead: 'Here are several alternatives based on your goals. Alternative A stresses the goal for low-income housing, alternative B the goal for rehabilitation of the commercial area...' and so on. The impact of each alternative on various facets of town life must be described. There are usually three or four alternatives – if there are more than three we planners lose our shirts! At Princeton fertile minds demanded the generation of alternatives without end. They argued, mainly among themselves and interminably. Every meeting lasted until midnight. The planning process was drawn out far beyond the schedule and in the end, not much happened. No one ever said community participation was easy. But in theory you start with very broad alternatives and narrow them as you find the range of feasibility. In order to give the community a way to decide, you produce a matrix that describes the impact of each alternative, by a series of categories. Then you say 'You decide' and leave town for six weeks. As they debate the alternatives, they build themselves a planning function that can be in place and tested when the project is completed. I tell them (using Bob Mitchell's ideas and words) that I am an itinerant hit-and-run city planner and when I am gone my plan will be shelved unless I leave behind people who can carry on.

Washington Avenue, Miami Beach

Washington Avenue, in South Beach, Miami Beach, is the heart of what's now called the Deco District. We named it, we were the first to suggest that Miami Deco architecture was a world resource. But South Beach was also filled with the old and the poor. Washington Avenue, the main shopping street, is a wonderful Deco environment, but very rundown. People here stop you and ask what you are doing and where you're from. They are mainly old Jewish people retired from New York, many of them are garment workers' union members; Miami is a last resting place of this historic Eastern European immigrant group. Here again you can see succession-invasion at work. Cuban restaurants jostle kosher delis on the Avenue. Some of the Cubans are Jewish. There are Ashkenazy and Sephardic synagogues among the storefronts on Washington Avenue. Because many old people live on government payments and on medicaid, storefronts house 'medicaid mills' and advertise that you can get your blood pressure taken for a dollar. Now the rich are moving in.

Our planning efforts should do three things for a community: help set up a democratic planning process; produce a fine-grained analysis of community characteristics, from demography to parking meter locations; and make urban design and planning recommendations that use our best imagination to make up for the lack of money for community development. Few communities can afford to pay for more than two of these three activities so, if I must choose between them, I will skimp on the analysis because after some years of working on Main Street I know much of what the analysis will show. It will show *inter alia* that the most convenient parking for customers is pre-empted by storekeepers who park in front of their own stores. Nevertheless, we made a careful analysis of Washington Avenue stores and their owners. The smallest storekeeper was also one of the most verbal. He had a store about 14 feet wide called Kid's Stuff. He rented cribs and high chairs to grandparents when their grandchildren came to visit. We considered the economic role of Washington Avenue in the region, pressures for change and growth, and the future of Miami Beach in the world economy.

In proper social-planning fashion, we produced several alternative broad-scale policy recommendations. Within these, our physical proposals for the Avenue were those we felt storekeepers could afford. We recommended mending and repainting the signs, restoring the Deco decorations when there were enough of them left, and replacing store awnings. Striped awnings and the painted signs and decorations on the stucco fascias above them should, we said, be the theme of storefronts. We made public sector recommendations for sidewalk and street improvements. We were forced into including trees. I don't believe in trees in front of small stores because they hide the signs and the store windows, and storekeepers cannot afford that. But we recommended a species of palm with a high trunk so the fronds would be above the signs. We recommended a more extravagant landscape (a Hollywood interpretation of a Miami landscape) for the traffic medians at the centre of the street.

Washington Avenue is a long street with fractionated ownership. The detail this required in our studies and plans was difficult to read on our maps; and the people who came to the meetings were old and couldn't see or hear well. We heard them say too loudly 'I can't tell what they are saying'. No one seemed happy with our proposals. I began looking around me in search of what pleased this community, then I realised it was the same Deco architecture that pleased us. The old people had come to Miami Beach when it epitomised glamour in the Hollywood of the 1940s. The 1940s picture postcards of South Beach Hotels, still on sale on Washington Avenue, were the elderly community's vision of Miami. I liked it pretty much myself. So I decided all our drawings should have palm trees and blue skies.

Hennepin Avenue, Minneapolis

Hennepin Avenue was a great white way in the hey-day of downtowns when cities still had money. With its rows of cinema marquees, it had been the entertainment district of Minneapolis and, indeed, of the mid-West between New York and Chicago. It was tawdry and seedy, a venue of prostitutes. Yet new office buildings were developing nearby it along Hennepin's trendy sister, Nicolet Mall. It was clear that Hennepin Avenue could go from great white way to 'grey flannel' corridor, although the honky-tonk would remain. Minneapolis had arrived at a principle they called 'hooker hydraulics'. This meant that if you push them off one street, they will come back on another, so it would be better to keep them where they are. Therefore we had red silk petticoats and grey flannel to deal with on the same street, as well as pleasantly solid masonry buildings from the turn of the century, honky-tonk, and the cinema marquee remains of the great white way. A further complication were the Minneapolis skyways that take shoppers and office workers between buildings above street level. These private corridors cross the public streets and are linked to form a public route that runs through stores and office buildings – one more variant on the theme of public-private relations.

We recommended that the white way now be produced in the public realm. We evolved a 'sparkle tree' to line Hennepin Avenue as it ran through the entertainment district. These tree-shaped, metal torcheres would beam big lights from their bases on to reflectors in their branches. Being public, they would be white and grey, not coloured; they would light the area but also provide a festive design framework, within which the neon of the private sector could go its own way. The skyways, being private, would continue the neon theme of the private buildings, yet have a more flamboyant, more public character. At night the sparkle

trees would read as white against the skyway neon. The grey flannel entrances of the corporate office buildings we kept discreetly on side streets.

We made separate sets of design guidelines for grey flannel, old masonry buildings, honky-tonk and skyways: four sets of parallel guidelines for one street. If you don't do that your urban design will be of limited use.

Republic Square District, Austin.

In Austin, Texas, we were hired by a developer to make a plan for part of an old warehouse district where he owned land. Our work as planners included proposing a site for the Laguna Gloria Art Museum for which we were to be architects. The Republic Square District was the site of the original town, platted on the river in 1839. The grid plans of small western towns are marvellous things. It's over simple to say that grids are simple. They give all kinds of options through their dimensions and rhythms, their orientation, and how they relate to the landscape. The Austin downtown was moving south and west toward the warehouse district. It was an area suited to large-scale change as it contained no housing and provided few jobs. The warehouses were mostly nondescript, single-storey buildings of the 1930s and 1940s.

Austin loves its natural environment and its lake. Unlike the rest of Texas, Austin has a smallness ethic. The trouble is that Texans love the smallness so much that they flock to Austin. How to remain a small town was a big problem. I won't describe our plans for Austin but will show you some of their symbols. Some are Texan, for example the lone star or the cowboy; some are southern, to do with the Civil War; and some are particularly of Austin, the Capitol or the live oak. We enjoyed, too, the combinations: the Capitol and the Long Horn, the Lone Star with the Statue of Liberty. Victorian buildings in Austin look unusual to a Philadelphian (or a Londoner). They are not the russet and plum colours we know, but are of a beautiful cream-coloured stone that glows in the evening sun. Austin public landscaping intrigued us too; it was a Texan adaptation of an English Romantic landscape, using live oaks.

These are some of the unique qualities of the city that we tried to address in our plans. We discussed Austin's symbols and the special character of the city's architecture and landscape with the steering committee and at public meetings. We find that people are often fascinated by our outsider's view of their city and grow enthusiastic about the heritage they have to build on and what it could become. When designing the Laguina Gloria Art Museum we turned for inspiration to the local cream-coloured buildings. We discovered that Cass Gilbert and Paul Cret, outsider-architects before us at the University of Austin, had melded Mediterranean and local influences to produce a lovely, cosmopolitan, Austin institutional style.

Centre City, Memphis

Memphis is set high on the bluffs above the Mississippi at one of the few locations where the river doesn't flood. Settlement is on the east bank only. On the west is a flood plain. Memphis is one of the few cities I know where you can look out from your office building window and see farm land. Where we in Philadelphia see Camden, they see green fields. Cotton used to land at the Memphis riverfront. Especially wide streets were included in the grid so the mule wagons could heave the cotton bales on a diagonal up and down the hill to and from the warehouses.

The imagery of Memphis includes not only the Mississippi and steam boats but also the parallel with Memphis on the Nile. The pyramid is perhaps an over-used symbol. Then there is Beale Street, the black main street famous for the blues and the blues musician W C Handy. Elvis Presley, too, grew up (in public housing) in Memphis and, some say, learned his trade watching

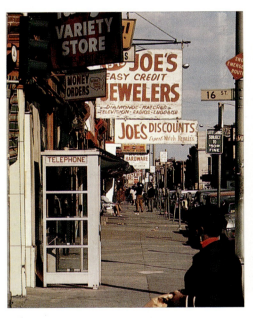

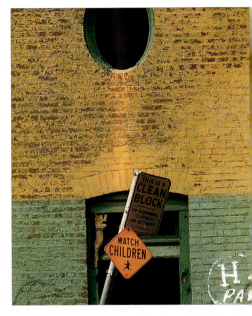
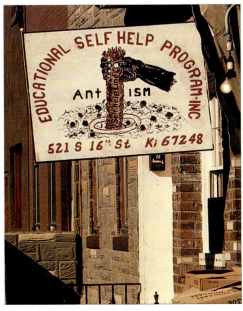

STREET VIEWS OF SOUTH STREET PHILADELPHIA

black musicians from the backs of the black nightclubs on segregated Beale Street. There is also the imagery of cotton and the cotton warehouses. Guess who's moving into the cotton warehouses? Architects of course. Then there is the famous Peabody Hotel with its fountains and ducks. The ducks waddle in and out from their rooftop home every day, while trumpets play and tourists applaud.

Yet all is not well downtown. The decline had already started with post World War II suburbanisation. In the 1950s and 1960s efforts were made to redress the decline through urban renewal and the introduction of expressways. Expressways and clearance for renewal destroyed traditional urban patterns and decimated the downtown. When Martin Luther King was killed downtown, rebuilding stopped for ten years; the city went through paroxysms of guilt and self-questioning.

In the late 1970s interest in downtown was re-kindled. A local family acquired the Peabody and regenerated it, making an elegant, sophisticated hotel. That was the beginning of something new. In the Peabody atrium civic events were held beside the duck fountain. People who hadn't been downtown in years came for the new chic. Soon after, gentrification started. A Deco cinema was converted to a civic auditorium, cotton warehouses became loft apartments and studios, new riverside housing was built, artists then architects then lawyers moved in town, and there was the beginning of a resurgence in office and hotel growth on sites near the river.

With the developers came financial organization and political support and a public-private Centre City Commission was instituted with powers to plan and finance. Their organization hired us. I set up a team of economists, transportation planners, cultural planners, social planners, landscape architects, preservation planners and local architects – we were eight consulting entities. We hired a minority consultant when a black Commissioner refused to vote for the planning study unless we did so. I was happy to do this and we found an excellent one to help us gauge the social and economic impact of our plans on the minority community and to build minority recommendations and requirements into the plan. To have such a consultant is necessary but unusual in downtown planning. Work was divided into eleven subject areas and seven major tasks. Over the three years of the project we gathered and analysed data and made recommendations, studying all subject areas in parallel and co-ordinating our work with each other, our steering committees and the public as we went. We left time for the steering committee and the public to consider our reports and debate the alternatives before getting back to us with their choices. As prime consultant, I was responsible for the overall planning strategy, the organization and co-ordination of the project, the urban design plan, one sub-area plan and portions of the housing, preservation and implementation plans. I edited all reports and wrote about half of the study's 21 volumes.

The map of the Memphis region shows that by the time our study was initiated major growth had taken place to the east, making downtown on the Mississippi the western boundary of the city. Within downtown, the original plat of the 1819 river town still existed, much eroded by the expressway and demolition. Beale Street, to the south, stood high and dry in a sea of clearance, as it if had survived a bombing. Although the publicity photos showed it alive with lights, Beale Street had been gentrified and prettified out of its former vitality and its new tenants still awaited an economic upswing. Main Street had been converted to a pedestrian mall, which probably accelerated rather than prevented its decline. The historic Cobblestones, where the cotton landed on the Mississippi, served as a parking lot; it had about it a strange air of abandonment, as if it, too, was about to be demolished.

When our study was initiated growth was starting along the river. There was new and rehabilitated housing, several high-rise buildings were in erection, and more were planned. The change in scale the new towers imposed was the immediate cause of our study. People felt the beauty of the location on the Mississippi could be lost, and with it, the economic advantages of downtown. They wanted a strategy plan to guide growth in good directions over the next 25 years.

We began by documenting the many facets of downtown's social, economic and physical development. We diagrammed the growth of Memphis from cotton port, to railroad town, to expressway city, showing how the bluffs had impeded industrial development on the river, leaving a soft river edge at the centre of town. We analysed uses and users of downtown. Our cultural planner made fascinating studies of the locations of jazz clubs and their users. Two of our three economists were former architects – in the planning we do it helps to have economists who understand and like old buildings. We made urban design analyses of the architectural character of centre city and its sub-areas and documented the connections – 'linkages' – between activities and districts in centre city. We showed problematic lack of connection, between downtown and the Mississippi, the north and south ends of downtown, the various renewal projects and Beale Street and the rest of downtown. We recommended desirable linkages between the elements of downtown and, putting these together, suggested the vitality the city should have. We sketched the directions in which centre city would be likely to grow and showed how these related to historic areas. We caused concern by placing on one map all existing centre city expressways and all those for which funding had been committed. This left one small link of an expressway ring still to be built, the portion that ran along the riverfront between downtown and the Mississippi. Seeing that plan, people were not convinced by the reassurance that no expressway was contemplated.

From the analysis we evolved a set of alternative development strategies based on three different views of the economy. Each encouraged and attracted growth but channelled physical change away from vulnerable historic districts and toward areas already cleared for growth. Each contained sub-alternatives for the riverfront, the mall and Beale Street, and there were also several transportation alternatives, including our recommended 'darning and mending' alternative. In transportation planning there is the 'macho' approach, which rams expressways through the city, and the 'feminist' approach, which employs many small-scale ameliorations to make maximum use of existing roads and avoid, as far as possible, the destruction caused by freeways. We usually recommend the latter. (The terminology is personal.)

We discussed the atmosphere and character of the civil rights museum, which will be a memorial to Martin Luther King at the Lorraine Motel, where he was killed. We made indicative plans for the shopping complex that will join the Peabody Hotel to Beale Street. This plan was intended primarily as a description of what the city should require of the new development to ensure it connects with and supports the surrounding activities of the city. We suggested that new housing built off-shore on Mud Island have a suburban, not an urban, image to make it competitive with suburban east Memphis. We worked with the minority consultant to establish community requirements to be met at the same time as support was given to downtown's plans for commercial and high-income housing expansion.

Finding something in the plan for everyone and dealing with all aspects of growth, not just architecture, have been the great challenges of this project. I wish I could tell you it was going to succeed. If you want to ask me during the discussion why I think things are not going well with community architecture I would be happy to tell you.

LAS VEGAS, STREET SIGNS

DISCUSSION

Martin Pawley, Simon Jenkins, Robert Thorne, Jake Brown, Ken Powell, Charles Jencks, John Thompson

RT: Denise has taken us a long way from the Hesketh Street Co-op and Lea View and Black Road, Macclesfield, and made us think about community participation in other ways – in so doing she told us a bit about herself and about the way she works with different communities in America – and introduced me to a number of words which I had never heard before – 'socioplastics', 'hooker hydraulics' – I will be using that at work tomorrow. I am going to ask Martin Pawley to start off in response to Denise's talk. Martin will be known to all of you as the architectural correspondent of the *Guardian* and the King of Technology Transfer.

MP: Thank you. I did think that my image as a kind of flame-thrower of community architecture could be applied this evening. I now realise after Denise's fascinating presentation that it is completely inapplicable. We are talking in terms which are quite different from one country to another. When Denise shows us plans of the re-development of the central area of a major city, I don't think it really can have the same name of 'community architecture' as the renovation of small houses in a small town in a very small country in a corner of Europe. I always used to think myself that the most distressing thing about community architecture in the last few years is that it was ironic that 20 years ago, we used to build 500,000 houses a year and think nothing of it, now if three people take five years to renovate a house in, shall we say, Macclesfield, several films are made about it.

Now, this is really, I think, the difference between these two things: between working with communities in the United States of America and self-help building boot-strap operations. Of course, I admit that that is an American term but self-help building is on a very small scale in Britain. My view of it is of course that bad design goes with community architecture, bad technology also and finally bad faith, in that community architecture simply doesn't do the job it's supposed to do. It is not a substitute for the construction of half a million new houses a year, any more than repairing old MGBs is a substitute for selling a million Ford Coronas. These are different problems which are still going to be approached through magnitudes. I don't frankly understand how the dealings with minorities, the dealings with poor communities in American cities which are described in a loving way by Denise can actually be compared with what we regard as community architecture and to what community architecture in this country thought of as its task. This seemed to me to be utterly different. There seems to be in America a confidence in the planning system, beyond that, a confidence in the legal system, beyond that, a confidence in the goodwill of everyone concerned, you can't say is present in this country. That is not the way we carry out our business. We are suspicious of our planners and don't trust our lawyers, there is a lot of trouble with the private sector, we don't like that either. It is very difficult to compare the two.

DSB: That's a romanticised view of America.

MP: Well, I was gong to use the term 'romanticised' and to say that what I propose about community architecture myself was that we should go 'cap-in-hand' to the Mitsubishi corporation or Honda and say 'How can you do this and sell it for a reasonable price?' That of course, doesn't refer to what you have talked about tonight, which is not, I think, an equivalent to taking three years to repair a house and then making a film about it. Four years to stop an expressway, a master plan of 25 years – these are statements of confidence, these speak of a realm where community architecture as conceived in Britain does not rate. Things have already gone beyond the point, all that stuff has failed before community architecture, as I understand it, is brought into play. With the best will in the world, I cannot regard this work as the same as the kind of work that Ron Hackney and the other people who followed him have done in this country because, as you know, I regard that as totally unsuccessful and based on a fundamentally wrong premise. So, that much being said, Denise, I thought it was terrific.

SJ: Can I just comment there Martin? Because I knew that you were totally unsympathetic to English community architecture, I thought that, if you could accept the great optimism and confidence of Denise's talk, you would therefore be extremely sympathetic to the way she was thinking about cities and about the way cities work. Is that the case?

MP: I have in fact lived in the USA for six years and I have been to most of the places she showed. Denise is a wonderful photographer of course, and you could take quite different types of photos in Las Vegas, showing the epitome of misery and despair in a totally heartless economic system. Denise talks in an upbeat, optimistic way of the kinds of co-operation you read about in newspapers in America which are not working at all. She talks about a 25 year plan that in 25 minutes is rendered useless by some change in the law, some political or sociological movement which wasn't part of her brief.

DSB: Can I say something to that? I did call it 'the rise and fall' and I have taken you up, I didn't have time to take you down. Community planning of our sort is having a very tough time in America. My plan may not be used and I could tell you the reasons in Memphis which would be general for the whole country. It would be romanticising to say that planning is done much better in America. Planning is like a haunted house since we have had Nixon and Reagan. The level of support and funding in many planning agencies is so low that people like me can't really work with them any more.

MP: But you continue to work with them

DSB: I may not do another plan because I couldn't afford to lose as much money as I lost on this one.

MP: But Denise, you didn't have a hard word to say about anyone in your presentation. Everybody was a good guy, they were all terrific and everything was working fine.

DSB: The point is that I tried to show you the essence of what I think democratic community planning should be. But, as I say, it is very difficult to do this kind of planning any more. Martin is right, the Memphis plan, like most plans, does depend in the short run on the outcome of elections, but its ideas are out in public, and this is only the first of its 25 years. We don't have time for a discussion of what happened to American planning and planning agencies in the 1970s and 80s but its conclusion would be that planning is no more respected in America than in England. In fact, maybe less.

RT: Well, let's come on to the fall later on. I am going to ask Simon Jenkins for his response. He is the Vice Chairman of English Heritage and therefore one of our leading conservationists.

SJ: I am in almost as an embarrassing situation as Martin Pawley because I find myself very rarely in agreement with him about something and in fact am surprised to find myself worried about some of the things Denise was saying. The gist of her presentation was political rather than architectural. I am always intrigued as a non-architect whenever I go to architectural presentations to see how absolutely fascinated architects are by politics and how bored they seem by their own profession. Here we have once again a fascinating political talk in which the architectural component was significant by its absence. However, the real question I would like to put to Denise is what I think is a central confusion – if not of community architecture (which I totally agree with Martin Pawley, is such a confused concept that it is better to remove it from the agenda completely and talk about planning and architecture, which is what the real subject is, and not befuddle our minds over definitions) . . . there does seem to me to be a central confusion in what it was that Denise was saying in aid of her approach. It was the attempt to find out what it is that 'People want to see happen to their environment'. Now there is no doubt that the movement that she was describing from the 60s into the 70s and certainly into the 80s to re-define the

showed them how they could use tourism, but not too much tourism for fear that it would alter the character of the old town. Now I don't think that it is terribly difficult, it is quite easy to evolve a system of planning which freezes the city or freezes a town. You can simply say that nothing will change here. We all know what that means, it means that the town ages.

I was slightly surprised at, dare I call it, Denise's naivety. When she went to these meetings, she was slightly surprised to find that most of these people were elderly. But it is not surprising that that they are elderly, these are areas which have reached the end of a cycle of change, where the occupants have grown old and where those old people do not want any more change. They would rather like public money to come along to restore the fabric of the city in precisely the way in which they want it. Now, I actually like many of the things which were thereby proposed, most of them are conservationist. I on the whole like the architecture they are trying to save and I am very sympathetic to it. But it leaves us totally defenceless against the forces of change. She ended up by saying that she had a much more pessimistic message to give us which she didn't get around to. I believe the message of that approach to community architec-

LAS VEGAS STRIP BY NIGHT

political process of planning has led to a far greater concern with 'what local people really want'. This has been the great strength of the Conservation Movement. It has been able to rely on a new sort of politics in towns to support itself, usually independent of the party political process or formal political process that, as is often said, legitimises planning decisions, usually in the direction of very large scale development. We can at least all agree about the famous traffic and highway engineers who never go by without a term of abuse. I was interested time and again, in her descriptions of the processes she was recommending for the towns. There were meetings at which local people came along and said what they wanted. An immensely complicated and traditionally American professional way of interpreting these decisions was translated into a new way of renewing the town. What these people actually wanted was that nothing should change. They wanted to see existing buildings, but more importantly the existing uses and existing occupants of those buildings continue. They wished to see the renewal to be essentially a cosmetic renewal in which the existing patina of the town was retained. In her recommendations to the people, I think of Jim Thorpe, Pennsylvania, she used a very interesting phrase, she

ture is very pessimistic. Most people want cities to change organically, slowly, if you like, but must accept the fact of change. We have got to find a much more radical way of channelling change and enabling it to take place, enabling new uses to come along without destroying the fabric which, I believe, as a passionate conservationist, is the adaptable element in a city which none the less retains its character. One thing I think slightly made my point: Denise spatters her remarks, as many architects and planners do, with derisory references to yuppies and the rich and new people coming into the area, but most of the slides are of precisely that happening. She shows a warehouse in Memphis into which architects have just moved. She doesn't really like the fact that they have re-done Beale Street, but actually the architecture is quite nice. Underlying it, is the fact that we rather like going round Covent Garden although we ritually deplore the fact that it is no longer occupied by the dear old biddies who used to be there 25 years ago. This naivety, this confusion, is central to urban renewal and I just don't think it has yet been resolved.

RT: Denise, are you instinctively an opponent of change? Are you an ally of the old folk?

DSB: I feel that Simon has misunderstood me because of the way I have had to focus my lecture owing to lack of time. In Jim Thorpe, what Simon says is true. Our plan was for the historic district, not the whole town; for about 5,000 people. It needs to be the way it is and the old folk need to live out their lives there, though there are young merchants and artists and middle-aged people in the historic area too. The problem was to suggest re-uses for the existing architecture with a little infill but not too much. Change will happen in the region, and this will change and intensify the uses within buildings in the town. This is, in fact, happening. Ten years ago there were nine functioning business on Jim Thorpe's main street, today there are sixty. The new market has come from regional growth. On South Street, however, there was considerable change. The antique row and restaurants that preserved the store fronts at the eastern end have prospered and so has the Italian market, because there's been an increase of upper-middle income residents in the city. To the west, residential growth has spread across South Street and well beyond. The city should be grateful to the community activists who stopped the expressway, if only for the extra taxes the growth has generated. Thanks to Alice Lipscomb, the low-

at how many people in their 70s and beyond came to meetings and in what fine fettle they seemed. In America, this is unusual and in Miami Beach it is still remarkable, as the numbers of old people are shrinking. This brings up the question of yuppification or gentrification. I agree with Simon that this is a central, unresolved problem of urban renewal, and was so long before the names were coined. I don't believe our proposals were naive on this question. There are degrees and we try for a balance. We search for means (very hard to find) to allow local residents and low-income people and sometimes artists, to reinforce their positions, usually through some form of assisted housing, *before* change takes place. We try to ensure that they will share in the prosperity, through finding jobs, when changes happen. In Miami we tried for a slow rate of change to match the rate of change of the elderly population, which was not renewing itself in South Beach. In Memphis, we got the (watchful) approval of the minority community for yuppification. It was a negotiation. They said 'We realise that this city needs an increased tax base and more employment. We will support your sponsoring housing for the rich and a large new shopping centre if you will support us in the renewal of public housing, and in our minority

LAS VEGAS STRIP BY NIGHT

income community secured some subsidised housing just off South Street, before land values rose too steeply. Community activists and preservationists got less than they wanted, though perhaps more than they expected, from the change.

In Memphis, too, despite the catastrophic earlier change, more large-scale change of a positive nature was welcomed. The need here was, precisely as Simon says, to find ways of accommodating change without destroying precious urban fabric. Our main strategy was to separate areas for growth and areas for preservation. We recommended channelling intense growth toward those already-cleared areas best located to receive it. In the historically and architecturally important areas we recommended infill growth and intensification of activities within existing structures. We had separate design guidelines for the sub-areas of the centre and for parts of sub-areas that would change at different rates. All our strategies were meshed, but particularly our transportation plan was co-ordinated with our preservation plan to provide highest levels of accessibility to areas of greatest change.

No, I was not surprised that there were old people in South Beach – how could I be, they are so famous – but I was surprised

affirmative action and community renewal programmes.' On this basis I gave my backing to the gentrifying elements of the plan. I felt too that they could bring employment. But I pointed out that the community should choose economic re-uses that could bring the types of jobs that gave the prospect of economic improvement for the low income inner city community; and that, with the jobs, should come support for education, so people who are there now will have the skills to get the jobs and to progress with them. I tried to find sponsorship for a branch of the local community college on the mall, where it could give courses in hotel administration, business and health services. These were all ways to help local low-income people benefit from the growth. Then in our indicative designs for new projects we showed where connections between old and new should be made. We tried to ensure that the new would support the use of the old. I am certainly not in favour of only maintaining what exists. Old and new, poor and rich, there should be room for all.

RT: I think we should now invite everyone to pitch in on this extremely interesting topic.

Jake Brown: I would like to say one or two things very quickly. Speaking of the English, when a word starts being used by politicians, it means that which is being described is finished or in acute crisis. As soon as the word community was used in this country, it was 'on its way out'. Of course in the last ten years there has been this systematic destruction of every sense of the word community because community is an intensely subtle and long developed thing of psychology, a form of interaction between people, of gender, of influx of other races and other cultures. What is marvellous about community is that it does manage to manifest itself against enormous odds. People can live in acute physical discomfort and circumstances if their cultural diversity is allowed to blossom but of course what we are doing in our cities is destroying even that. The cities are in such tremendous crisis that the main connection now, the main physical connection, between America and this country, is that the city of Philadelphia is sending its trash and New York is sending its rubbish to North Wales. This is a measure of the world crises of which the city crisis is a microcosm. Consequently, there must be a profound reappraisal of what happened. What I would like to comment on, and I agree with Martin, is that what we are seeing in this country is a masterly English way of dealing with crisis where a theatre is played out. What we have

with us. I think that I was cheered by the lecture, if a little bit worried because what one had was definitely a positive message that the cities could live and that hopefully, despite Reagan, Bush and Quayle, they presumably aren't about to erupt. The worrying aspect was I suppose qualms about the paternalism of planning and really was this going to work in the end better than the last time?

RT: Charles Jencks?

Charles Jencks: Well I was fascinated by the personal aspects of Denise's past in getting into this subject. I was also impressed by Herbert Gans' theories and writings. These seemed to have played a great role, which I think she underplayed because of shortage of time. This notion, which has been evolved in America is not familiar in Britain, that any urban culture which is large will be made up of many different taste cultures, five or six in a large, ethnically varied American city. What struck me as interesting, if at the same time philosophically strange, about the presentation was that Denise's sensibilities and values seemed to come from the AA, from the 50s, from the Independent Group, from Nigel Henderson's photography. More often than not, she favoured a taste culture which, if one puts it in the terms that one

 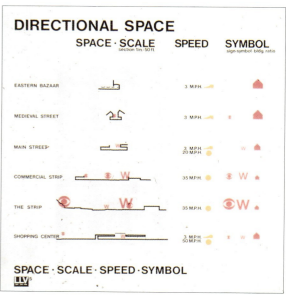

L TO R: SHOP FRONT CHURCH, SOUTH STREET, PHILADELPHIA; DIRECTIONAL SPACE DIAGRAM

now is the Theatre of Community Architecture with two Hamlets, Prince Charles and Rod Hackney. People do want things to change, what they want is a certain natural and inevitable and desirable quality to their everyday life with some level of peace, some level of security, some level of reasonable residential scale. They all know very well innately what they want. When they see these things taken away and destroyed, they don't want them taken away and destroyed, they are not resisting change, they are resisting the ruthless, unthinking technological exploitation of themselves.

RT: Thank you. Ken Powell, did you think that anything that Denise was saying struck a sympathetic cord? Kenneth is the architectural correspondent of the *Daily Telegraph*.

KP: I just felt at the end that one was seeing just another kind of manipulative planning, happening perhaps in a wonderfully American way, being very progressive and achieving things . . . and I do actually feel that American cities still have something going for them (so do British). Cities are lively and positive places. Really this seemed to be an example of eternal American optimism similar to what we were hearing in Britain many years ago, the garden city ideal of the LCC seemed to be actually still

has to adopt in Gans' terminology, is a kind of lower-middle-class taste culture, in other words, the poor working-class taste culture of the blacks. Now Gans says in his defence of this kind of approach, 'Well basically everybody else has perfectly good representatives, enough money and a proper acknowledgement of their taste'. So therefore it is necessary if you are going to be a socially conscious professional, to represent the under-represented taste culture. The problem with this, as I see it in your presentation and your asides, which I think you would admit are derisive toward the yuppies and towards the rich and towards change, are that of course all of the people in any class system or in any taste culture have a dynamic relationship with other taste cultures. One level of this is to want to be like another taste culture and emulate it. In a sense what your designs show is favouring of Mid-America, the pop graphics, the Henderson social realism. You are favouring a kind of lower-middle-class taste culture. I was interested in one aside where you said 'Well we give them the grey flannel too'. In any good city, you have to have many levels. Now, I would like to hear you talk about your personal feelings towards those other taste cultures. Why put them down? Why not give them an equal validity? Or are your feelings so strong that you think that one is better than the other or more socially valid?

DSB: I love those old warehouses and I think what the architects have done with them in Memphis was often very good. At the same time, I recommended real suburbia for Mud Island because I knew it would draw some people that downtown needs to help revive it economically. Our designs weren't what some architects wanted there. They would have preferred the housing to look like the Thames Embankment. But I tried to do a middle-class suburban environment very well. As an urbanist, my recommendations must combine prediction with design. I can't merely say, 'This is what I want'. I must say, 'This is what I would recommend within what I think you are likely to get, based on who is going to design and develop it'. Representing the interests of my client, the city, I must tell them the implications of the acts of others or of the acts they themselves are contemplating, 'Given that, this is what you are likely to get, and this is what you should ask of them, in aesthetic and social terms'. So, as an urban designer, I try to act responsibly toward all tastes, but I do have personal preferences. When we did our Learning from Levittown study, I loved most the ethnic housing

civic buildings, you have to satisfy several taste cultures. You can't design for only one group. City hall must have something for everyone.

CJ: What I don't understand is how you decide which taste cultures to favour? When you have a conflict, which do you in fact favour?

DSB: Well, in civic architecture, you try not to favour one or the other, you try to find what they share. In British society, in American society, there are vast numbers of shared values, otherwise the mass media and advertising wouldn't work. Messages have meanings, not just for narrowly profiled groups but for large groups. In America, for example, the TV situation comedy 'All in the Family', is one that straddles a great many taste cultures. In it are young and old people, liberals and conservatives, blacks and whites; the whole lot come together. You could say that it is a bland and pallid hodge-podge. Yet we do respect art that appeals to many tastes and classes. We now know that Shakespeare didn't appeal to a broad audience. It was a romanticism to think that he did and Shakespearean scholars are now saying that his plays weren't, in fact, enjoyed by working-class people. But Verdi was. So, there is great art that

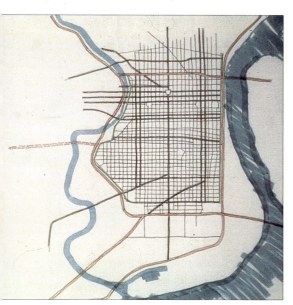 

L TO R: SOUTH CENTRAL TRAFFIC PATTERN; SHOP FRONT, SOUTH STREET, PHILADELPHIA

of South Philadelphia. Although I would never design them as an architect, I found the decorations Italian-American South Philadelphians applied to their houses the most interesting and amusing and, in a strange way, after my own heart. How you accommodate different tastes as an urbanist is not to say 'I like this type of brick, therefore *you* should use it'. That is not your role.

My role as an urbanist must be different from my role as an architect designing a home for a person, meeting them across a table looking into their eyes. I can have a great fight with my client about taste at that level. Predicting how the big new shopping centre is going to be designed by the developer's architect, then saying to the city: 'Out of this design, here is what you should try to draw' is a very different task. I don't go all the way with Herb Gans in his prescriptions for sub-cultural programming. Herb says that taste cultures should hire architects from their own culture to design for them following the taste of their culture. That doesn't work on two grounds, first, if someone who lives in a Levittown house hires an architect, they probably want to change taste cultures, and may not appreciate hearing the architect say 'I like the house you are living in now.' Second, in

does reach across taste cultures and great art that doesn't. If you are doing large-scale civic work, you should look for the art that does. Of course time enters into the equation. Many people hated the Eifel Tower when it was first built.

John Thompson: It's interesting how annoyed people get about this wonderful term 'community architecture' but I think this proves that it is going to be here a lot longer than a lot of people would like to see. I think a lot of people have had their heads down in a trench in fear of seeing another television programme about community architecture. These programmes actually reach many, many people not here tonight but who are in fact suffering at the hands of people like ourselves, planners and journalists. There are people who, through seeing programmes about community architecture on television, want to support the role of people in all professions who are actually getting to understand their environment. I think people are confused by the difference between community architecture and community enterprise, so much so that they have probably been misled by *The Times*' RIBA award, which is an enterprise scheme that a lot of people think is community architecture. I think that nobody can deny that community enterprises are a good thing; politicians of every party believe they are a good thing, be it Marxist power-to-the-people or Thatcherite self-help. So I think we ought to forget community enterprise and let's see whether there is such a thing as community architecture. If so, where is it and who is practising it? I was fascinated by your talk this evening because it seemed to me that you were talking as a planner who was taking a holistic approach and whenever you were confronted with a problem you went out to find out what the problem was. You didn't say, 'This is where I stand, this is my theory'; you went out and devised democratic, participatory processes, as far as you were able, to find out the nature of the problem and the nature of people's needs and then you added to that knowledge your own skills as a planner. Now our profession is not generally interested in doing that, our schools of architecture and architectural journalists are much more interested in those architects who are either pursuing their own careers, or who are interested in technological innovation or those who are in pursuit of intellectual ideas (it does not matter what intellectual idea, as long as it's rigorous!) What community architecture and community planning is about is finding an architecture which is always appropriate and meaningful for that particular situation. An architecture which is not palpably removed from people and with which people can find a rapport. It's not a style but it is, I believe, a process which we certainly believe we practice on a very wide scale both in New York and New Hampstead. It doesn't have to be an instituted architecture, it doesn't have to lead to slavish conservation, it doesn't have to patronise the proletariat. But I think it's the architecture that we desparately need and I think that it is the architecture that will one day be realised as the movement that is on-going. It needs definition and I don't think it should be swept under the carpet. I think that there are communities out there that, when they actually get the architecture, can tell the difference.

DSB: It's difficult, without knowing much of British community architecture, to know 'where you are coming from', so of course, I put my own meaning into what you say. I think you're right that communities can tell the difference. I would be wrong, though, to leave anyone with an impression that all this is working in America and that because I've suggested solutions, they are going to happen. I want to leave you with an understanding that I'm optimistic in one sense, but pessimistic in another. I think I've done the best job I could of getting democratic participation and deriving, from the technical skills of my colleagues and myself, something that would make sense for the community, and not doing it manipulatively. But in each of these projects there's been disappointment. On South Street, for example, once there was money to hire staff planners, we volunteers were squeezed out of the process. And of course we couldn't get an ideal democracy and of course the process got awfully drawn out, as it was in Memphis – now the 21 volumes are out, who's going to read them? I included a long list of who should read what; but is anyone going to read my list? And I haven't got the money to call and say 'Please make sure that so-and-so reads that one'. Troubles mount. The Centre City Corporation was funded largely by fees paid by developers. With little development going on, there's little money; so who's going to sponsor the plan? I keep telling myself we'll have to build support for the plan slowly, but at the back of all of this are two words your can't use in America today – Tax and Liberal. Yet if no one will pay higher taxes, we're not going to be able to help the worst problems in cities and this has been going on for years now. On South Street when we worked there, you could still buy an abandoned house for about $10,000 and you could get a grant, if you were a low-income person for $3,000. But there was no way that $3,000 could bring the house up to code, so you could occupy it. So all the self-help in the world, even with that grant,

wasn't going to fix the house up. We were stuck with the fact that, even with the programmes that were available and the equity people were prepared to use, there was still a big gap. Perhaps in Britain too the resources for community architecture still leave too big a gap, and that's the problem Martin talks about, that you need millions of houses to solve the shortage.

MP: Very briefly, I can't let the subject pass without addressing John Thompson. One thing that he forgot to mention, something that was prominent in one of his own press releases, was just the incidence of smoking amongst the people who have lived in the properties which have been done over by community architecture. That's just an aside. I'm sure there's another side to the coin. I feel that, just looking at this, the difference between the American assumption of the term (and what's happening in America has been beautifully illuminated from the floor) was far clearer, certainly, than when I was confronted with the horror of speaking after Denise had finished. But I do think that there is an issue concerning architects here that could finally perhaps glue all of us together and that is that community architecture, in whichever way we view it, is a kind of euphemism for an 80s term for social architecture, which, of course, as Denise said, has a much longer history. And social architecture, as Jake Brown said, when you take it seriously, is ultimately an immense global technical task. And my question, really, about British community architecture falls into two sub-questions: one, is it not really just another way of finding accomplices to go along with the crimes of development; and the other, is it really what people are trained seven years to do, when the task that really confronts us, in the global resource allocation, in the technical sense, is so much more urgent?

SJ: I still find that I'm agreeing with Martin Pawley, which seems to worry me. But listening to Denise and listening to the contributions by other architects, I keep feeling that architects are out of their depth here. This is an area where they've strayed, out of frustration, with the particular planning regulations of this country and they've decided that if they can't best them they'd better join them; and in joining them, they've found themselves endlessly knocked over by huge bulldozers: to wit, urban capitalism, big city government and big central government. I do not share the conventional view of many British architects that everything is glorious in America because they can build the buildings they want. I find American cities, on the whole, less nice places to live than British cities – I emphasise the 'on the whole', I also think that the triumph of British politics – of British architecture and politics – is our planning system and I think our planning system is, on the whole, better than the American system. And many Americans think that too. Now I wouldn't carry that thesis too far and I wouldn't claim too much for it, but I would go at least as far as that, and therefore question the general assumption that America has this wonderful self-confidence, this crash-ahead approach. I've been to downtown Memphis and I think it's awful and I'd rather live in most equivalent-size British cities, for all the faults that we have in those cities. The advantage we've got is that we've learned how to make rules to govern planning. We have all sorts of problems in trying to make those rules constantly responsive to what, not local people, but the generality of people, want out of their city as it changes. I'm nervous about architects coming forward and saying 'I'm just a link, I'm just a connection, I'm just translating what this particular group of people are up to who turn up to my meeting and say what they want to the people who are going to make it happen'; because the people who are going to make it happen are very sceptical of that approach. I share Charles Jencks' scepticism about style here. I'm reminded of Kenneth Brown's evocation of all British cities, which involved awnings, trees and seats. Awnings, trees and seats are one architectural solution to urban renewal and I'm sure that it's one that many people at a public meeting would like to see. But, it's not the only one, nor is it necessarily validated by a public meeting. I come back to my original point, which is that I'd like to see architects confine themselves to building nicer buildings. The architect was trained to enable the building, either an old one being reconditioned or a new one, to respond to a client's wishes. I'd like, occasionally, at sessions like this – where I have to be slightly pompous – to hear more talk of this.

AFTERWORD

I have claimed a lecturer's *droit de seigneur* to comment on the overall of the proceedings at the Tate Gallery. To me, the most fascinating part of the talk was the discussion afterwards. I think we were all, even when the comments sounded contentious, actually comparing notes. The comparisons were between practice in England and America, between architecture and planning, and perhaps between evolutionary change and revolutionary change. The discussion was intense because we all face the dilemma of wanting more than the on-going systems will provide, for people, cities and architecture.

Although I smart at being called naive and confused by Simon Jenkins, I feel he best illuminated our conflicting aims: wanting to preserve beautiful and historic cities yet realizing one cannot turn one's back on large-scale change; wanting to produce housing and environments for all people yet needing the support of the rich and powerful to do it; feeling outrage at 'capitalist bulldozers' (socialist bulldozers too) yet realizing that flower-pots and awnings are not the answer to urbanism; wanting to be an architect and finding oneself drawn into politics in order to be a socially responsible architect. I feel Simon's debate is as much with himself as it is with me. If he becomes an alter ego in what follows it is because his points are so cogent. Pawley gets his turn a little later.

Simon, on occasion. transfers from his experience in England, which is not mine in America. For example, not only old people, nor even mostly old people, come to our public meetings. He makes derogatory remarks about democracy by public meeting. I agree that at public meetings are little old ladies in tennis shoes, kooks, crazies, people with hidden agendas, special pleaders, architecture students and rabble-rousers. But so are true citizens, patriots for the city, and those who want to see things happen. People who attend public meetings are the shock troops of urbanism, the ones to pound on the mayor's door. Granted they are not a representative sample of the residents and workers of an area and that we must make contact with these too, yet I have found that, despite this cast of characters, public meetings can proceed more rationally than one might think. 'Sit down!' will be heard in the hall and, to me, 'You don't have to listen to what she says, she *always* says that'. This is because people who attend public meetings often know each other well or know the system well and police their own crazies.

Nevertheless, because the direct democracy of public meetings is biased through self-selection, we try as well for a representational democracy through interest groups, as I have described earlier. We introduce the appointed or elected citizen steering committee to the members of the city agencies they will be working with, and try to help them form a *modus operandi* that will continue beyond the plan. But there must also be other means of reaching citizens. Perhaps the media are the most important. Community groups that survive and prosper become adept at involving the media, especially television, in their causes. Beyond this, every community has its points of contact; possibly a storefront on Main Street, a newsletter, drop-off points at important institutions. The implementation report for the Memphis downtown plan suggested many of these.

The forms of democratic participation that I sketched in my talk must increase in complexity with the size and scale of the area planned for. Because our early experience was working with the denizens of one street or of quite small communities, we had a rude awakening in Minneapolis when, despite the acceptance of our plans by the steering committee and an approving vote in City Council, others higher in the urban heirarchy and not part of the planning process debilitated the plan. A visiting architect told a large-scale property owner the plan would be bad for property values. In terms of our instructions from our client, we had no recourse to these people to explain. Also, some ambitious artists decided they would rather do the design. Although they had not been to the earlier public meetings, they accused us of not observing democratic processes and of not showing alternatives. We were, they opined, theorists; they were better designers. I felt this was a good example of people with their own agendas using the mechanisms of democracy for an undemocratic purpose.

As the community increases in size so the face-to-face group grows unwiedly and representation becomes the means of achieving democratic participation. Here the democracy is, of course, not as direct; but representational democracy's strategic grasp on the larger unit suggests that, at the larger scale, it can produce more for communities than can the town meeting. There is a continuum between direct and representational democracy or between centralization and decentralization in government; where along the continuum governmental planning can be most effective is a subject of debate among political scientists. The location of this point must be established for each community at the outset of the plan, usually by trial and error; therefore provision should be made both for co-opting additional members onto the steering committee and for holding extra meetings as the true shape of the community becomes evident in planning.

So this is two cheers for democracy: for our cultures the best but not a perfect system. Yet in the multi-level interaction of community planning I have never felt that I am 'just a link'. If I have won the trust of the community, I am expected to recommend and to say why I recommend and I will be listened to. I may not get everything I want, but I find, perhaps particularly in low-income communities, that there is much more support for the artistic aspects of planning than the social planners thought there was. The only time my drawings were ever called 'master-pieces' was on South Street.

Simon feels architects should stick to architecture and wonders why they turn so easily to politics and ignore design. The social planners, too, felt architects should stick to architecture, but they were criticizing architects' insistence on proposing physical solutions to economic and social problems. Demolishing much of downtown Memphis to make way for *Ville Radiuese* was considered by the social planners to be the fault of architects. Unfortunately the social planners dictum was heard by the

Post-Modernists as good reason for abandoning social concern in architecture, 'Architects can't help so let's not try'. This, it may be gathered, is not what Bob and I intended. It is ironical to find oneself categorized as 'too political' in London where we have also been accused of providing socially irresponsible 'vulgar American pastiche'.

Having first accused me of politics, Simon later seems to lay the demolition of Memphis at my doorstep, despite the fact that the methods I have described were evolved to try to avoid just the architectural bias and social ignorance that led to the spoliation of the city in the first place. In my talk I spoke as a planner *and* as an architect. Presumably as a planner I should be aware of politics and should understand in what sense 'the personal is political'. Certainly my training has prepared me to take care of more than architecture in urban planning. I've talked about architecture on many other occasions and shall again; the evidence suggests that I care quite intensely for the art of architecture. Like the circus horse rider whose horses diverge, I try mightily to draw my two professions in parallel paths; but you *do* change hats when you change from planner to architect, the question is of degree. My complaint with many architect-

complexity that I have been discussing.

Is there no room for design in community architecture and planning? I believe that where there is least money and greatest lack, greatest architectural imagination is required to bring needed beauty out of severe restrictions. This may be a romanticism, yet I feel that most architects who learn to think in this way will become better architects.

And yes, urban design does have to do with politics and it does have to do with ' awnings, trees and seats' and with flowerpots (although I am against flowerpots on Main Street) and with the broad range of urban building that lies in between. Mostly urban design has to do with the linkages between all of these and with the connections between the urban disciplines. It demands the ability to bring appropriate physical conclusions out of complex urban subject matter. Yet once you begin to think in this way you may also design a better doorknob. Yes, architects should build nicer buildings, and they certainly should respond to the needs of their clients (I thought I was talking about that) but when they do urban design they should not treat it as large-scale architecture. And I agree that architects must know their architectural trade and agree there is a particular problem that urban designers often

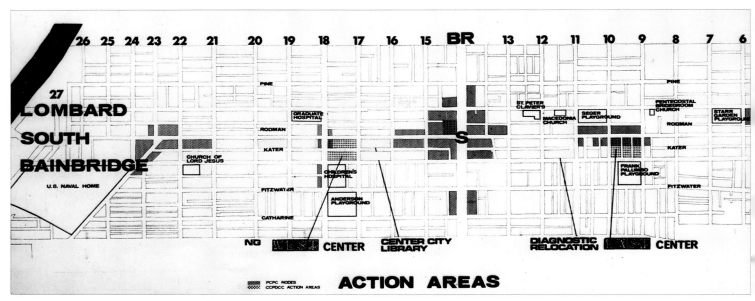

ACTIVITIES MAP SHOWING EAST AND WEST CENTRES, SOUTH STREET, PHILADELPHIA

urban designers is that they can't make the change. They merely design large-scale architecture.

If architects are not to be politicians should they be sociologists? 'Certainly not' I used to say when I trained architects in urban design, 'we don't want to *be* sociologists, we want to use the material of sociology for an urban design purpose'. Without doubt the sociologist can't do this for the architect. Many sociologists can't think in physical terms. So the architect has two problems: one of communicating with sociologists in language that will allow them to give answers, and the other of translating those answers into their physical correlates. However, Gans has pointed out that on occasion architects must indeed be sociologists as well, simply because there are not enough sociologists to serve all the problems of urbanism and particularly of housing. Yes, of course, architects should do architecture. But some problems cannot be dealt with architecturally and architects must know how to recognise these problems and, when necessary, to respond to them in non-architectural ways. Not all architects need to learn to use sociological imagination; not all architects need work at the scale of urban design, but most architects can benefit from learning some of the

don't: it's no use bringing a rhetoric to a community meeting, the community has more than enough of that already.

I am not among those Americans Simon mentions who prefer the British planning system. The British respect for the civil service must make life much easier for British planners. However, I agree with my social scientist colleagues who look with awe upon the powers accorded planners in England, and with amazement at the unsophistication with which the powers are used. American planners are more philosophical about their task and more aware of its complexities than are English planners, perhaps they have to be because in America planners are given much less leeway for action. An unfortunate recent trend is that urban designers are now being accorded considerable power in American cities, for a complex of reasons too long and too macabre to describe here. One's hair stands on end at the decisions these architects-turned-urbanists make.

I agree with Martin Pawley that the problems of housing go far beyond the reach of community architecture into areas of national strategy. But I strongly disagree that the issues are primarily technological, or that the solution will lie first in approaching Honda and Mitsubishi or, as we used to say, Ford and Taylor. The myth of mass production has haunted the field of housing for more than fifty years. Architects have the fantasy that houses can come off the production line as cars do (or did – the days of the tin lizzy are over on the production line too. Thanks to computers, they all come off different.) The reasons why housing can't benefit from automobile production techniques are multiple. Because construction is not more than one-third of the cost of the delivered house and lot, the industrialization of construction will achieve savings on only part of the cost. The major costs in housing lie in land, codes and regulations, labour organization and project management. The great savings are to be made through rationalizing some of these, to some extent through size, but perhaps more as the Levitts did, by vertical co-ordination of the sectors of the housing industry, to gain control particularly over materials availability and delivery. Perhaps Martin should turn his attention first to the fact that, at least in America, the housing construction industry, unlike the auto industry, is regionally based, atomistic and fractionated. Houses aren't built like cars and the industry today is not set up to compete in this way.

The popularity of mobile homes may seem to refute these

creativity won t lie first in design. Most of the housing measures that have worked have been economic and legal; they range from giving tax incentives to supporting non-profit housing groups. With political and economic support for affordable housing, technological innovation will follow. Unfortunately technology can't lead and, after fifty years of hoping, architects should abandon that pipe dream and (*pace* simon) deal with the messy here and now of housing policy.

John Thompson pointed out that my talk was more about community planning than community architecture and that therein lay the real difference – more than the difference, say between the United States and the United Kingdom. He's right. However, our discussion covered architecture and planning, and I approach this topic as both architect and planner; therefore, on balance, my title holds.

I agree with John that community architecture is important symbolic activity around the problem of housing. As he points out, it raises the level of awareness in a population that otherwise cares little for housing the poor, and it is therefore a first step toward bridging a gap. Community architecture attracts princes and poor people; and it produces photo opportunities for a good

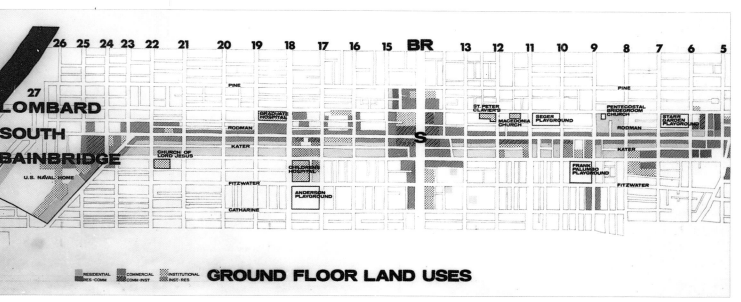

GROUND FLOOR LAND USE MAP, SOUTH STREET, PHILADELPHIA

assertions. (What do you call these in England now? They were called 'caravans' but language has changed so much that I feel like a piece of archaeology when I am in London.) Mobile homes achieve their primary savings through the lower unit cost for land, the higher density levels they are permitted, labour savings and the removal of the requirements of codes – sometimes to the extent of creating firetraps. For such reasons mobile homes can produce important savings and a considerable portion of the American housing market is now served in this way – without the aid of architects. Architects' attempts to co-opt the mobile home industry have again produced no more than fantasy. I feel Pawley's parable of the role of the arcades in giving us CADD is more pertinent to this problem than the work of Cedric Price or Archigram, or than Martin's flinging his cap into the Honda ring.

The real problem that architects' production-line romance skates on top of is the scandal that the majority of Britons and Americans, being adequately housed themselves, care little that some fellow citizens lack the very minimum. The answers to this problem lie, unfortunately, in changes in public opinion that will permit the devising of well-funded, system-wide housing production strategies. Strategy planning needs creativity too, but the

cause. But without further support the gap between housing supply and demand will remain scandalously unbridged. The political will is needed first. Perhaps a prince can help achieve this, but architects can't be more than stagehands in this drama. As it becomes obvious what must change, the limits on what princes, communities or their architects can do will be equally obvious: voters and ministers must turn the problem around. Thereafter technologies will follows; they could even include those Pawley wants, so long as the caveats I have mentioned are understood.

The fact that five houses won't help solve the housing problem is not a reason for doing nothing at all. Unfortunately many architects today have taken Pawley's criticisms as good cause for turning away from the problem altogether. Before that, advocacy architecture served, on occasion, as do all pieties, as the last resort of scoundrels and a haven for the inept. The strident manifesto hid the bad architecture. But this, too, is no reason to abandon. Heave on community architects, social planners, conservationists of broad vision, transfer technologists with horse sense, architects of uneasy conscience and good will; is that the creak of the pendulum I hear, swinging our way?

the grand proletarian cultural locomotive LLV

the grand premiere to the world   A&A   10 Jan 69   10:00 a.m.

'LEARNING FROM LAS VEGAS' POSTER FOR THE JURY OF THE LAS VEGAS STUDIO

CONCLUSION

ELEVATION, PEABODY PLACE AND BEALE STREET, MEMPHIS

This profile has been an effort to push the architectural pendulum in what, I feel, are some needed directions. To do so, I have dwelled on urban 'paralipomena' that could serve as muse for architectural artistry, and have explained my ideas by pulling apart then piecing together the fragments of my professional life. The brave times I recalled at the beginning of the story are long over. Some of their ardent protagonists are gone. Robert

Scott Brown, Paul Davidoff, Margherita and Franco Paulis, William Wheaton, Giuseppa Vaccaro, and Reyner Banham died at too early an age. Others like Arthur Korn and Charles Seeger have left their friends joy in their long, productive lives. My student, the Central American architect, is a venerated professor; Herb Gans has gone 'back' to sociology and I have perhaps gone 'back' to architecture. I have tried to be true to the selves I have developed in three disciplines and three countries, although the attempt to define the resultant professional identity floors me. Visits from overseas colleagues and my working trips to London have brought spiritually valuable opportunities to integrate the centrifugal forces of my career.

Our fields have been less susceptible to integrative discipline. Architecture has subsided into a series of flurries and eddies; there are no broad currents that could be defined as a school. In the United States planning has dispersed and public sector planners have sought new homes, casualties of the trend to the right and the starvation of public agencies. Urban design continues to slither insignificantly between planning and architecture. In all three it seems high time for a return to social ideals, though perhaps the best we can hope for is a 'kinder, gentler' professional world.

I started the task of pulling together through a survey of cross-Atlantic influences. At the end, the audience at the Tate Gallery went a similar route, comparing English and American experience. Although we were able to find much that we held in common, a great deal was different. I discerned, as well, stereotyping and prejudice. What I said was defined by those who spoke afterwards as can-do American optimism. A perhaps not wholly justified smugness was evident in, for example, the comment, 'It may well be the case that the sorts of buildings thrown up in America may indeed reflect the difference in confidence and the difference in style culture (whatever that is)...' The speaker meant 'taste culture', but seemed not to have known the term. The African in me sits this one out, concluding with George Bernard Shaw that the English and Americans are ·separated by a shared language, and marvelling at how strong the emotion still is. As I see it, American culture diverged from the start from the British. Quite how different America is takes time and study to understand; a year spent in Manhattan won't do it. The critics were confused because they couldn't basically accept this difference – their norm for America is England. The 'is' of the mother country is still the 'ought' for the colony. Yet, as Norma Evanson said to Aldo Van Eyck, 'There are things *we* know are wrong with America you haven't even heard of

yet'. Paradoxically, American architects and critics remain colonials of the mind: if I want my ideas read in the United States, I will do well to publish them in Britain.

Luckily on other axes we can meet as people. I hope the tradition of humanistic urbanism that I have tried to describe will be intriguing and morally appealing to architects and that some will share the aesthetic and intellectual excitement of planning and urban design considered as nurturing for cities. In 'urbanism with a human face' the roles for architects are many, but they demand an understanding of the differences between them yet, in the end I understated what is required of architects in the city. As I watched my friend Barbara Capitman struggling to preserve the Deco District of Miami Beach, I saw her rely on her parental heritage in the arts, her childhood experiences of great European hotels, her training as a journalist, her professional work in social and economic research, her study of trademarks, her interest in gerontology, her knowledge of Jewish culture, her understanding of the 1930s and 1940s – all these she threw into trying to save the Deco District. The city needs all you have and are.

Paul Davidoff once said that architects who feel they can design everything from a teaspoon to a region have delusions of grandeur, and I agree with him. So I am bemused to find myself working on projects that span from the millimetres of jewellery to the miles of the Manhattan waterfront, and on everything in-between. As an architect and planner, not an architect-planner, urban design is one way, not the only way, of using my skills. Although it is my joy to open many windows onto my world and my pride to know when not to design, for me, all turns eventually toward the tasks of design; architecture remains my own window and my chief means of focusing my probably too discursive professional life.

Then the question arises, 'As an architect, what *did* you learn – not from Las Vegas but from social planning, urban planning, and urban design'. The best answer is, 'See our work'. But read also Venturi's description of our approach to the planning of museums (the 1987 Cubitt Lecture, the *RSA Journal*) and consider whether it isn't a translation into architectural terms of what I've said here. Defining architectural problems as broadly as we would urban problems will lead, we hope, to buildings that complexly serve and express their uses, their communities, and the aspirations of their times. This is nothing new. good architecture has always done this, and the city, by contrast or analogy, has always provided a point of departure and a proving ground.

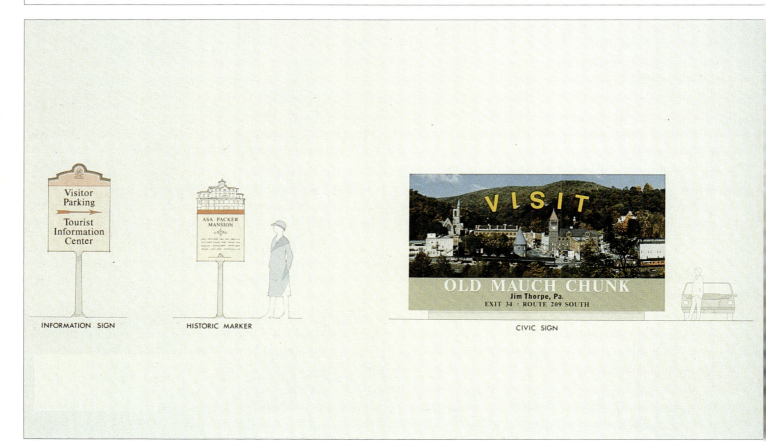

ABOVE: RECOMMENDED FACADE AND STOREFRONT IMPROVEMENTS. *CENTRE*:RECOMMENDED STREET IMPROVEMENTS. *BELOW*: SIGN PROTOTYPES

GENIUS LOCI OF JIM THORPE
Pennsylvania

RECOMMENDED BUILDING AND SITE IMPROVEMENTS

Jim Thorpe's image derives, from its past virtue as the thriving centre of the coal mining industry, and its present state as a treasury of proud, faded, underoccupied structures witnessing both its former prominence as an industrial centre and the subsequent obsolescence of its economic base. Its evocation of bygone glory and its spectacular setting create a romantic and picturesque image.

A particularly unusual feature of Jim Thorpe is that the physical structure of the town is still largely intact, probably owing in part to its tight integration with the land and the constraints imposed by topography on new development. Steep mountain walls enclose the town in a narrow winding valley running east to west. The Historic District is almost totally enclosed by the valley and beyond by the mountains to the east. Disconnected from its obsolete industry, that once fronted the river and Susquehanna Street, it is inwardly-oriented. With no cross streets, the densely built main street, Broadway, is the central corridor of the town and follows the bends and turns of the valley. Two secondary parallel streets serve additional tiers of building on the south valley wall. In places, built form, rock terracing, and retaining walls are almost indistinguishable from natural rock outcroppings and the valley wall itself. In the interlocking of land with built form and in the distinct definition of its shape and limits, Jim Thorpe is utterly unique. It is beautifully, ingeniously and relatively unalterably engaged in a difficult and spectacular site, and remains a place where natural elements still remain as the focal features of the landscape.

The formal organisation of Jim Thorpe allows us to understand its social and economic history. Asa Packer's mansion, on a hillside at the edge of the town, underscores Packer's prominence and dominance. Elaborate brick residences on Broadway and wood-frame working homes in The Heights reveal both the

prosperity of the coal and transportation industries and the social ordering of the town. The buildings of the Lehigh Coal and Navigation Company, the Courthouse, and the Jersey Central Railroad Station, set in a triangle at the entrance to town, attest their importance by their location, architectural quality, and magnitude, and signify the town's pride in its achievements.

Jim Thorpe linked coal mines in the hills to the west, to river and canal transportation, and later to the railroads. It was truly a centre where all aspects of the region's industry and all those involved in the industry converged. But the atmosphere today is permeated with a feeling of obsolescence and lack of purpose. In Jim Thorpe today, Blakes vision of industry's 'dark Satanic mills' encroaching on pleasant pastures as is poignantly dated as are the remnants of the palaeo-technic industrial era that abound in and around the town. Coal mines, canal and even the railroad, now in decay, seem to form part of the Romantic landscape, even part of the very American wilderness they once stood against. Symbols of human battle against an overwhelming nature now seem to return themselves to nature as Romantic ruins. Quantities of vacant space exist in the town that was once not only a bustling industrial transfer point, but also a showplace of the prosperity flowing from coal. The streets where captains of industry once mingled with in the miners and on the bargees are almost empty now.

The problem as we see it, is to restore serviceability in the present within the unique and visually fragile framework that developed in the past. Our effort would concentrate on the interaction of the image, associations, and atmosphere of this heritage with new uses and activities that would restore economic viability and renewed purpose in the present.

In delineating the relation between a unique jewel-like town with a proud industrial heritage, the canal that once served it, now mellowed and softened with time, and the extraordinary landscape that determined the character of both; we can explore the reuse of historic physical connections, as well as structures that were vital to the region's early history. History here can be viewed not just through a single artefact or piece in isolation, but contextually as the use of the land, places, technology and lifestyle developed in relation to each other.

Jim Thorpe's chief architectural value to us today is that it is an almost intact and undisturbed community of the Victorian era. Its buildings span the 100 years of the American industrial revolution that brought power and wealth to the community. The town was built most vigorously and continuously from the 1850s through the 1890s; the Victorian era produced modest domestic, institutional, and commercial buildings with occasionally inventive and remarkable examples of the Vernacular, Gothic Revival, Italianate, Romanesque, Queen Anne, and Shingle Styles.

Along Main Street, 'Broadway', the elderly descendants of the Welsh and Irish miners live side by side with young family groups, part of a recent immigration to the area. It is for the benefit of this local community that we have addressed issues of commercial revitalisation and historic preservation in the Lower Historic District of Jim Thorpe with the hope that economic revitalisation in this core area of high visibility and historic prominence will have a positive impact on the District itself as well as on neighbouring areas and nearby communities.

On the one hand, the District can be viewed as a remnant and museum piece unconnected to area-wide land use developments. Alternatively, the District and the uses of selected adjacent lands can be viewed as parts of a larger cultural and recreational resource which require an interdependent analysis and development in order to conserve and best use places of historic importance, scenic beauty, and outstanding recreational and cultural appeal. The Historic Jim Thorpe study takes this latter point of view hoping to demonstrate that by giving 'revitalisation of historic Broadway' a larger context, greater vitality and economic opportunity can result.

With this approach it is not necessary to make of Broadway one more 'Victorianised' Main Street, 'preserved' within an inch of its economic life. When viewed in its regional context, with its broadly based, still evident historic identity as the vital nexus of historic regional transportation and industrial systems, there is no need to Victorianise the Sunrise Diner or the Sunoco Station. Their difference lends spice. In this sense, our plans should help Jim Thorpe use the assets of its heritage to become more vividly, what it already is.

Three topics of concern emerge as *foci* of our study: historic preservation, commercial revitalisation, and outdoor recreation and tourism. Significantly, the town's realisation of the need to plan its future has coincided with a growing national interest in historic preservation, neighbourhood conservation, downtown revival, energy conservation, and ecological problems of the natural environment.

It has coincided as well with a greatly spurred participation in outdoor recreation and other tourist activities located within a few hours of major metropolitan areas. Opportunities in each of these areas naturally overlap and mutually reinforce each other. In downtown Jim Thorpe, in the Mauch Chunk Historic District around Market and Hazard Squares, a rich stock of Victorian architecture is now much in need of an infusion of new retail commercial uses. Many of Jim Thorpe's historic landmarks – the Railroad Station, St. Mark's Church, the Asa Packer Mansion, and George Hart's Steamtrain Ride – are already tourist attractions, drawing visitors from area camping grounds as well as daytrippers from Philadelphia, New York, Allentown, and New Jersey. The annually increasing volume of visitors here could easily be persuaded to patronise some new lively uses in the downtown. Moreover, the possibility of linking the three areas of concern in terms of marketing, tax benefits, rehabilitation financing, and employment, portend the success of preservation and revitalisation opportunities in the Lower Historic District.

We have steered away from Jim Thorpe's development as a nostalgia piece, a museum, a literal restoration that would stop time and entice only tourists. Instilling new and varied activities to improve its economic base would go further toward renewing the town's sense of purpose and community than solely addressing the superb physical qualities of its past that form its existing character. While trying to revitalise physically its serviceability in the present, we have not relied on the capricious grafting on of gimmicks and exogenous elements – malls, kiosks, and street furniture – but feel the character and history of the town would be better served by a regard for current use patterns and needs, by careful maintenance of existing structures and renewal of active use within them, and the thoughtful location of new forms.

Physically, many techniques and approaches exist for preserving, interpreting, and communicating history, some literal, some

AERIAL VIEW

not. Our approach physically is to blend elements of exact restoration of images of the past with impressionistic and incomplete suggestions of the past. Sensitively juxtaposing the old and the new, allowing the integration of new forms and images that accompany new functions, bringing out the essential character of each, and promoting awareness of both continuity and change through time is fundamental to our approach.

The total visual effect of the streets in Jim Thorpe should be enhanced through a variety of means involving restoration, repair, and renovation. The idea is not to promote pure historical restoration on one hand or pure modernisation on the other hand, but to enhance what's there now – to bring out the good qualities in what exists in this remarkably intact 19th-century town that, within an overall Victorian vernacular, includes a variety of formal and symbolic elements deriving from a diversity of building uses, hybrid styles of architecture and ornament, graphics and building adaptations. Our approach is: almost anything goes if it is good in itself and sympathetic to the whole.

The whole we speak of in this way will come from a complex and rich order made up of analogous and contrasting elements and styles. Among the analogous architectural elements along Jim Thorpe's facades are the materials and natural colours of the building surfaces, the warm, dark brick and stone walls, which conform to a 19th-century palette of sombre yet rich colours; the rhythm and scale of the architectural elements deriving from the uses of the buildings when they were built; the pervasive richness of ornament; the tight definition of the street by the building facades and porches; and the forested, enclosing mountains which focus and subordinate all other elements. Contrast along these streets derives from the moderately varying heights and widths of the buildings; diversity of architectural styles and ornament – windows, bays, doors, cornices, porches, balconies, and stoops; the judicious placement of major, large buildings at intersections and as focal points at bends in the road on Broadway; the occasional breaks in the building line giving slot views to the valley walls to the north and south; and the varying styles of renovations and colours of painted walls and trim.

The aesthetic balance among analogous and contrasting elements is often subtle and difficult to categorise; very much depends on the quality of the elements and their relationships. A brash Art Deco or Modern sign may look all right among the old late-Victorian facades or may not. In general, in the architectural configurations of Jim Thorpe, relationships are more successful when the formal elements are analogous to each other and the symbolic elements are contrasting. For example, Newberry's 5 & 10 on Lower Broadway has successfully integrated a modern store-front design and signage at street level within its Victorian brick facade. The renovation at the southeast corner of Race Street and Lower Broadway is far less successful aesthetically primarily because making a one-storey building look good as an infill in a row of three-storey buildings is almost impossible – it is among the hardest of design problems. Also, the new facade, in this case not stylistically analogous to its neighbours with its infill of panels of aluminium siding, is jarring in this particular setting. The major formal element the original builder omitted from this building is the storefront which in Victorian times, for a shed commercial building, typically consisted of an applied rectangle of wood clapboards, display glazing and an oversized cornice which stood higher in profile than the gable roof of the building. Property owners seeking to renovate stylistically indistinct buildings have a choice: they can restore their property 'as is' or they can look at the historical buildings around them for clues to appropriate, innovative rehabilitation solutions which meet practical building re-use needs.

Many of the small houses along Broadway have been stripped of their Victorian cornices, porches and decorative wood trim. Maintenance costs are thereby simplified but the replacement of original decorative features with ornamental colonial eagles and sconces from the local building-supply store wholly negates the original character of the home. Such personal touches can be highlights when they are merely a small addition contrasting with an already restored facade.

Buildings of outstanding stylistic and historic significance make an extra demand upon the owner for high standards of restoration and maintenance. Public sector maintenance is a necessary support to assure building owners and tenants that their renewal efforts will not be wasted.

Remnants of slate and brick sidewalks and granite curbing can be found throughout the Historic District. We recommend restoration if possible of the existing paving material, particularly if it happens to be stone or brick, by resetting, relevelling and regrouting as required. Concrete has long since replaced these materials in the majority of areas throughout the Historic District but even so, many of the newer sidewalks and curbs are in need of repair. Along the south side of Broadway concrete sidewalks have settled where their foundations have settled or have been washed away at the curb line. In general we recommend brick paving of varying patterns and granite curbs for public buildings and areas of prominence; ie Market, Hazard and Packer Squares. The high cost of using these materials prohibits their comprehensive use in other parts of the Historic District, unless this use is funded by private initiative. Sidewalks and

OF JIM THORPE

STREET VIEWS OF JIM THORPE

curbs should be carefully detailed. The colour and texture of paving and curb stones should be chosen to blend with brick facades. Urban scale, that undefinable quality much in evidence in Jim Thorpe architecture, will be lost if contrasts between sidewalk and facade or paving and curbing are too pronounced; or if curb stones are too narrow. Curb cuts for the handicapped and for vehicle access points to car lots should be carefully graded. For new curb work, especially in prominent areas of the Historic District, we recommend installing an empty underground conduit for future accommodation of lighting services.

Sidewalk entrances to the houses of Stone Row on Race Street are made of slate slabs which have been depressed and dishevelled by application after application of asphalt topping on the narrow street. A study should be undertaken to determine how to protect the houses from 'asphalt encroachment', either by providing curbing between road and slabs or by resetting and relevelling the slabs at a higher elevation. Public pathways and steps along hillsides and terraces need constant attention to withstand harsh freezing-thaw and drainage-erosion conditions, and the encroachment of natural vegetation.

Skillfully layed out pathways traverse Kemmerer Park below the Asa Packer Mansion and provide a leisurely grade change and pleasant experience for visitors and residents walking to and from The Heights. Decorative cast iron fences and railings along these public areas should be repaired, reset, and repainted. Pathways leading to hiking trails and public terraces should be improved and marked for visitors.

We recommend the adoption by the Borough of a Victorian period light fixture. An ornamental lighting programme is expensive and, like the use of expensive paving materials, should be reserved for public buildings and prominent areas like Market, Hazard, and Packer Squares, and perhaps Kemmerer Park. Cast-iron Victorian lamp poles and metallic halide illuminated period fixtures would provide a soft warm glow (at modern standards of illumination for public safety) for the important areas of the town. An ornamental lighting system provides a warmth and period ambiance both day and night that is inviting to visitors and residents alike as, for example, in Historic Bethlehem and Society Hill in Philadelphia.

Where street trees have already been planted, these should be left. Any new street trees should be restricted to areas between buildings and be set on lot lines where they can serve to mask parked cars. They should of course be used in public squares such as Packer and Kemmerer Parks where there is enough room for them to thrive and be properly maintained. Over the years, the streets of the Historic District have become wider and the sidewalks narrower. Where trees once stood in front of the American Hotel, cars are now parked. Congestion and maintenance problems would result from the planting of street trees along these narrower walkways. Isolated instances can be found where trees may thrive but a spotty streetscape would result. Visual relief from buildings is readily afforded by the spectacular views of the lush, carpeted green mountainside which wraps the town on all sides, as well as by the Victorian gardens along Broadway that can be seen from the street, through the narrow gates and passages between row houses, and from loftier elevations in other parts of the town. These private gardens and the use of window boxes produce an enchanted spell of beauty for passing visitors and residents and should be encouraged and perhaps celebrated by public tours at certain times of the year.

Recommendations for the initiation and installation of a public signage and communication system may be divided into parking, civic, directional, and interpretive signs. A further set of signs – banners, posters, leaflets, notices, and handouts – being transient, answers to different constraints and requires a further set of guidelines. All of these signs, being 'civic', must be differentiated from U S highway routing signs and markers on the one hand, and from commercial signs and billboards on the other. The character and image they should portray, whether it falls between the commercial and civic ends of a spectrum or lies on a totally different continuum, poses a nice problem to the designer. However, civic signs must answer to the same legibility criteria as all other signs. They must be readable, their content must be comprehensible at the distance and speed and within the cone of vision from which they are intended to be seen.

Signs at the entrance to town should indicate general locations of major attractions and where to park, signs near a chosen attraction should again locate parking; other directional signs should clearly indicate the site of the attraction; interpretive markers should give information on it, and further 'civic' signs, at pedestrian scale, and courtesy of local businesses, should tell visitors what goods and services may be acquired at walking distance from their cars or the attraction. (This helps to spread the benefits of tourism.)

To achieve such systemic consistency, the total communication system for Jim Thorpe should first be planned on maps of the region and the Borough. For the consistency to be apparent and the system to be usable on the streets, careful consideration must be given to the character of each type of sign. One sign type, the parking signs, should be differentiated from the others. This sign gives practical information. It should resemble highway marker signs in character, although not in colour, and all parking signs should be the same. The design of parking signs should be adapted from the Federal Highway manual.

We recommend the New York World's Fair cast iron bench for use throughout Jim Thorpe as a street bench. This is a pleasant and comfortable Victorian design that can in its own way identify Jim Thorpe. Alternatively, period designs, which could be produced locally and which meet high standards of design, can be used and manufactured under an area-wide programme to re-establish Victorian craft industries. New benches are always welcome at bus stops, on the south sides of major streets and under shade trees in parks. We caution against placing benches along a sidewalk of width less than six feet.

The policy recommendations that we have made above for the aesthetic treatment of Jim Thorpe will not rise above the level of good intentions unless they are related to means of implementation. However, moving from a believable myth to a workable reality, or to put it another way, from well-intentioned aspirations and prescriptions to policies and their implementation, is particularly difficult in the area of aesthetics. This is not only because tastes differ, but because the area of taste is qualitative and undefinable. The same words can be used to describe vastly different physical results and, in assaying the quality of these results, we are bound to depend on the discretion of judges to whom we have assigned the role of taste experts.

Extracts from Historic Jim Thorpe: Preservation and commercial Revitalisation, *a study of the old Mauch Chunk Historic District, made for the Carbon County Planning Commission in 1979.*

Carbon County Commisioners; Albert U Koch, *Chairman*: Charles E Wildoner; *Vice Chairman*: Bud Angst; *With the assistance of*: Pennsylvania Historic and Museum Commission, US Department of the interior, US Department of housing and Urban Development, Borough of Jim Thorpe, Mauch Chunk Historical Society, and Pennsylvannia Department of Transportation, District 50
Venturi Rauch and Scott Brown Architects and Planners: *Partner in Charge*: Denise Scott Brown; *Project Directors*: David Marohn and Mary Yee; *With the assistance of*: Eve Baltzell, Tom Bernard, David Brisbin, Frances Headley, Mark Hewitt, Arthour Jones, Missy Maxwell, Janet Schueren, James Timberlake, and Robert Venturi; *Economic Consultants*: Thomas P Reiner and Stanley Taralia

SITE PLAN, PRINCETON URBAN DESIGN STUDY

PRINCETON
New Jersey

STREET VIEW PRINCETON

College towns maintain a unique spot in our imaginations. Linked to our nostalgia for youth, they follow us and thereby send their image throughout the country. This is especially true of a university of world standing such as Princeton, whose context is international and whose graduates are traditionally widespread. But although the University is central to Princeton, the town predates the

University and part of its image derives from colonial Princeton, a post toen on the Kingston road.

Having developed over a period of more than 200 years, Princeton's physical character expresses its incremental growth. Yet there is a consistency reflected in the scale, texture, materials, and architectural detail of buildings and spaces in the Central Business District. These physical characteristics go a long way to describing the urban image loved by the community.

The late 19th and early 20th century architects of the University, recalling the Oxford and Cambridge of Gothic spires in a country town, chose English Collegiate Gothic as the style for the Princeton campus. In the 1930s, the designers of Palmer Square combined the Colonial post town image with the English university town image of academic courts and quadrangles set among bustling market streets. To extend the retail activities of the Central Business District, they placed an idealised version of a New Jersey Colonial square at the northern edge of the campus, at its point of greatest contact with the University. Post World War II, the Colonial aspect of the Borough's imagery was reaffirmed, as Princeton became a highly desirable residential and corporate address. Today, mundane problems cloud the image. Regional highways and suburban shopping malls, exert a decentralising pull on the Central Business District. Storekeepers in the Borough are nevertheless beset by parking problems. Heavy economic pressures accompany small but visible eco-

nomic failures. The country town is heir to the problems of the megalopolis. This study has been undertaken because there is hope that the unique character of their town can provide a theme to guide growth and a context for solving problems.

The Development Plan is a basis for protecting and enhancing the unique qualities of downtown Princeton life. At the same time, it provides for the economic vitality of the Central Business District. The Plan is much more than the sum of its parts. Its primary purpose is to see whether several important projects – a commercial expansion of Palmer Square (whose site plan was given), housing for the elderly, a library expansion and parking facilities – could be developed in a small downtown while protecting community values. The resulting Plan accommodates these projects so that they are compatible with each other.

The Palmer Square plan envisages that there will be an extension of the present square to the north to form a ring of commercial uses around an enlarged square. The building programme includes office space, retail space, an 80 room addition to the Nassau Inn, and 15 to 25 apartments. This space is contained within five buildings, four of which lie at the outer edge of the expanded Palmer Square ring street. These four buildings have retail uses at street level and offices on the upper three floors. The fifth building, the four-storey Nassau Inn Extension, is at the centre of the ring. It has retail uses and a public space for cultural and other community uses on the first

IMPACTS	ALTERNATIVES						
	I CBD PROJECTS AT ORIGINAL SCALE	II (Z) WITHERSPOON/ SPRING GARAGE MODIFIED	III (Y) PCH OUTSIDE OF CBD	IV (Ω) PSI SMALLER- WITHERSPOON/SPRING GARAGE MODIFIED	V PCH WITH GARAGE ON WITHERSPOON/ SPRING SITE	VI (X) PCH ON ENTIRE WITHERSPOON/ SPRING SITE	VII MINIMAL CBD BUSINESS DEVELOPMENT
URBAN DESIGN IMPACT	GREAT CHANGE IN CHARACTER	MODERATE CHANGE IN CHARACTER	MODERATE CHANGE IN CHARACTER	MODERATE CHANGE IN CHARACTER	MODERATE CHANGE IN CHARACTER	MODERATE CHANGE IN CHARACTER	SMALL CHANGE IN CHARACTER
NEIGHBORHOOD IMPACT	HIGHLY NEGATIVE	MODERATELY NEGATIVE	MODERATELY NEGATIVE	MODERATELY NEGATIVE	MODERATELY NEGATIVE	MODERATELY NEGATIVE	SLIGHTLY NEGATIVE
USER NEEDS	PCH-OK 120 PSI-OK 105,000 LIB-OK GAR-OK	PCH-OK PSI-OK 105,000 LIB-OK GAR-OK 1000	PCH-NO PSI-OK 140,000 LIB-OK GAR-OK 1225	PCH-OK 126 PSI-NO 55,000 LIB-OK GAR-? 1000	PCH-? PSI-OK 140,000 LIB-OK GAR-?	PCH-OK 109 PSI-OK 140,000 LIB-OK GAR-NO 925	PCH-OK 126 PSI-NO 40,000 LIB-OK GAR-NO
BUSINESS IMPACT	STRONGLY POSITIVE	POSITIVE	POSITIVE	MILDLY POSITIVE	POSITIVE	MILDLY POSITIVE	NEGATIVE
BOROUGH REVENUE	GREATLY INCREASED RATABLES	GREATLY INCREASED RATABLES	GREATLY INCREASED RATABLES	SLIGHTLY INCREASED RATABLES	GREATLY INCREASED RATABLES	GREATLY INCREASED RATABLES	SLIGHTLY INCREASED RATABLES
TRAFFIC IMPACT	HIGHLY NEGATIVE	HIGH/MODERATELY NEGATIVE	MODERATELY NEGATIVE	MODERATELY NEGATIVE	HIGHLY NEGATIVE	MODERATELY NEGATIVE	MINIMALLY NEGATIVE
DEVELOPEMENT DENSITY	HIGH DEVELOPENT DENSITY	HIGH DEVELOPEMENT DENSITY	MODERATE DELOPEMENT DENSITY	LOW DEVELOPEMENT DENSITY	HIGH DEVELOPEMENT DENSITY	HIGH DEVELOPEMENT DENSITY	LOW DEVELOPEMENT DENSITY
(PARKING IMPACT)		(522 FRINGE SPACES)	(375 FRINGE SPACES)	(171 FRINGE SPACES)		(519 FRINGE SPACES)	

PRINCETON URBAN DESIGN STUDY - VENTURI AND RAUCH - JUNE 26, 1979

ABOVE: LIBRARY PLAZA FROM HULFISH STREET; *BELOW*: TABLE SHOWING PLANNING ALTERNATIVES

floor with hotel rooms and apartments above.

There is a pleasing variety of heights and scales of buildings in the CBD, that relates to their uses and their locations. The limits placed on intensity of development in the CBD through zoning, floor area ratios, and height restrictions, have helped to limit the bulk of new development. In general, the existing differences between the large-scale buildings on main streets, such as Nassau Street and Palmer Square, and the smaller-scale buildings to the north of Nassau Street and on alleys, should be maintained. The range of heights and scales should not become too great, as this will disturb the complex balance that now exists. Bulky necessities such as parking structures should be located, *inter alia*, where they are least visible and will not disrupt the scale of main streets.

The scale of public open spaces in the CBD should be modest. Where new public open spaces are formed these spaces should be articulated by tree planting so that they remain in scale with the uses and activities around them and so that they do not attract extremely large crowds. In their detail, however, they should be sturdy and solid; their scale should be urban and suitable to mass use. There should be a difference in scale between the furnishings of the University campus and those of the Princeton plazas. Just as there are locations where bulky parking structures are least disturbing, there are also a few locations where other relatively bulky, but more visible structures may be tolerated. However, the architectural character should be the subject of careful consideration by the Borough and the developer.

The well known views and vistas of Princeton have to do with Nassau Street, with the meeting of town and gown across a tree-lined but busy main street. From Nassau Street there are inviting views north up streets and alleys and another famous vista across Tiger Park, toward the Nassau Inn. From the CBD there are equivalently beautiful views south toward the campus. Development and improvement in the CBD should be based on an understanding of the importance of these views to the image of Princeton; their potential should be exploited. The small streets and alleys off Nassau Street are particularly important. As they become the locus for more intensive use of space through rehabilitation, they should be helped to extend an attractive invitation from Nassau Street.

The provisions of the Development Plan will result in the formation of several important new vistas in the CBD. A view at an acute angle across Tiger Park will give an intriguing glimpse of the new stores of Palmer Square North. A view looking east along Hulfish will open up to include Hulfish Plaza. A small fountain in Library Plaza will terminate the axis of Hulfish Way, and the Princeton Community Housing Project for the Elderley will act as a backdrop to the Plaza.

In Princeton today there is a considerable difference in the character of different types of streets and open spaces. The difference, for example, between the character of Witherspoon Street and that of Vandeventer Avenue, between a tightly-knit commercial street and a generous and uninterrupted residential one, is unusual for streets in such close proximity to each other. The Development Plan proposes to extend this variety to include several open spaces, both formal and informal, all of which will be carefully tied into the activity patterns proposed for the CBD, to help support its economic and particularly its retail, functions.

As the major new development in Princeton is located so centrally, it is important that the architectural character of the Palmer Square extension respond sensitively to the theme introduced by the older Palmer Square buildings. We endorse the decision to maintain the height line and the articulated incremental quality of the existing buildings in the new addition. Building materials, too, should be carefully selected to go with the old. This is not the place for glass towers or metal cladding.

The present design of Palmer Square and its extension is based on the belief that, in order to draw retail and office activity north off Nassau Street, movement north must be encouraged and the movement system made easy and comprehensible. However, we believe that a strongly attractive activity should be placed at that northern end of the square to help anchor the small-scale retail activities there. This could be a strong cultural facility, or a large and popular store.

For the Palmer Square complex to exert an attraction from Nassau Street, as much of it as possible must be visible from the street and the view should be pleasant and framed. For this reason we have recommended that Tiger Park, in addition to containing a civic and cultural welcoming sign to Palmer Square, be treated as well as a gateway and a frame to the Square. We have suggested tree planting to separate the open space at Palmer Square One from Tiger Park, and further that the trees on Tiger Park be artistically pruned to lift their canopy so that there is a view of Palmer Square under them in the summer.

Princetonians have the opportunity to live in an environment that many people remember nostalgically from their youth, and that many more yearn for. People who live and work in Princeton know that the reality is somewhat different. The recommendations of this study are modest. They have been focused almost entirely toward trying to understand and support the image and the way of life that Princetonians, and very many others, want to see retained here.

Extracts from Princeton Urban Design Study, *for the Borough of Princeton, New Jersey, 1980*

Princeton Urban Design Study, *Design Date*: 1978: *Consultants*: Venturi, Ruach and Scott Brown; *Principal in Charge*: Denise Scott Brown; *Project Directors:* James Allen Schmidt, Mary Yee; *Project Urban Designer*: Frederic Schwartz; *With the Assistance of*: James Bradbury, David Brisbin, Barbara Friedman, Frances Hundt, David Marohn, John Rauch, Lee Rayburn, and Robert Venturi. Alan M. Voorhees and Associates, Parking Survey: *Deputy Vice President*: John F Callow; *Project Engineer*: John R Wroble; all perspectives drawn by Frederic Schwartz.

HENNEPIN AVENUE ENTERTAINMENT CENTRUM. *ABOVE*: BY DAY; *BELOW*: BY NIGHT

HENNEPIN AVENUE
Minneapolis

MAP OF STREET SIGNS

The towers on the Minneapolis skyline dramatically symbolise the city's role as a cultural and artistic, as well as a governmental, financial, and services centre. A city-wide effort has been invested in channelling and directing this growth, to ensure that overall urban goals are achieved in the process. Nicollet Mall and the skyway system – co-operative efforts between the public and the

private sectors – and a host of excellent new buildings are the result. This regeneration continues today. Development pressure from the city centre has moved out in several directions. New governmental and community institutions have been built to the north and the south. There has been commercial expansion to the east. To the west, even one block from Nicollet Mall, change has come more slowly. Land values drop off with surprising suddenness, and something has seemed to impede redevelopment.

To the west stands Hennepin Avenue, a long and historic Minneapolis street. For much of its length, it is an essential functioning part of the movement and land use systems of the region. But the portion of Hennepin Avenue that passes beside the central business district has enjoyed better days. Once the hub of entertainment for the metropolitan region, Hennepin Avenue has seen this function disperse to the movie theatres in the suburbs. Beautiful and historic movie theatres remain but not in their original use, and the function of Hennepin Avenue as an entertainment magnet and locus has been lost. Other entertainment uses have crept in, some of the 'adult' sort, and there has been regeneration of fine commercial structures on or close to the Avenue, for cultural and retail commercial uses.

Hennepin Avenue as it stands, is certainly not dead; it presents a lively though somewhat confused environment. It has a definite character and one that has great potential. As the Minneapolis CBD expands, this potential gains the chance to be realised. The

construction of the City Centre project between Nicollet Mall and Hennepin Avenue and the rehabilitation of the Lumber Exchange and the Hennepin Centre for the Arts will be a great force for change on Hennepin Avenue, signalling the probable end of the inertia that the Avenue seems to have exerted on development to the west. The block directly across from City Centre on Hennepin Avenue, Block E as it is called, is a certain candidate for redevelopment as a result of the City Centre project. Further new building and, as important, considerable rehabilitation, can now be expected on Hennepin Avenue.

These portents have been accepted by the city as a challenge to direct the forces for growth to the west of the CBD for the good of the city and the region. Thus, the city decided to develop a plan to help Hennepin Avenue achieve an identity within the city and region that will enable it to realise its potential to share in and add to the social, economic and cultural vitality of Minneapolis. A unique identity was established for the Avenue. It was to serve as a 'transit-entertainment centre'.

Transit use on Hennepin Avenue will increase considerably as office construction expands in the vicinity. There is the need to organise this use, and to provide amenity and protection from the weather. At the same time, the entertainment uses that still exist on Hennepin Avenue are vital to the culture of the city and deserve to be supported. An entertainment identity would serve to distinguish Hennepin Avenue from its neighbour, Nicollet

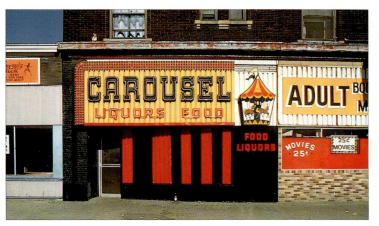

GENERAL VIEWS OF MINNEAPOLIS AND HENNEPIN AVENUE

Mall, and to give focus to the other uses that must be encouraged on the Avenue and to the amenities that must be planned for it.

The city was resolved that the planning team should not merely solve technical problems and functional requirements of the programme, but should also present a visual image in the spirit of a quality entertainment district and 'a design which is a leader both locally and nationally'.

To achieve this high level of design, a programme was instituted that required, in essence: a careful interdisciplinary analysis of the problems and a rational process of relating goals to means, choosing between alternative means of achieving goals, linking chosen means to form a plan, and developing this plan in detail.

The Urban Design Plan

Hennepin Avenue is not an orderly visual environment. Yet it has a vitality and variety that would be easy to lose and that are themselves valuable and important indices of urbanity. The variety is not merely physical. The physical variety represents a variety of uses available for users of different ages and tastes.

Entertainment uses range from first-run theatres to the 'adult' type; the span of taste cultures served is another index of urban vitality. The scale of uses is mostly quite small. This contrasts with the larger-scaled, more intense uses of the new buildings to the east. New-old, vital-orderly, finished-unfinished, changeable-unchangeable – these are elements of the contrast that give Hennepin Avenue identity. Large buildings, old and new, on the Avenue, form anchors of stability. Through their relatively more stable uses and solid construction they provide ballast, to the signs, symbols, transit uses, and 'adult' allure of other sections. The area we have labelled the 'Entertainment Centrum', stands in contrast with portions of Hennepin Avenue to its north and south, where newer, more orderly complexes terminate the bright lights. A natural boundary to the entertainment district is created at its southern end through a bend in Hennepin Avenue at Tenth Street. Land use change provides a clear definition at the northern extreme at Fourth Street.

The focus for the design is the right-of-way of Hennepin Avenue in the Transit-Entertainment Centrum, between Fourth and Tenth Streets. There is a broader 'study area', which serves as a context for decisions on Hennepin Avenue, and for which design recommendations have been made.

A major objective of the Hennepin Avenue Transit-Entertainment Study is to resolve several transportation problems in the Hennepin Avenue corridor. The large volume of traffic and pedestrians along Hennepin Avenue has created a serious traffic congestion problem which has resulted in a large number of accidents and inefficient traffic and transit movement. Of the top 30 intersections with the highest number of accidents in the City of Minneapolis, eight are located on Hennepin Avenue within the limits of this study.

Streetscaping improvements to the right-of-way span the complete length of the proposed beneath ground improvements and include portions of some cross streets; however, a greater level of investment is planned for the Centrum between Fourth and Tenth Streets. The transit and traffic improvements, the reshaping of sidewalks, re-alignment of traffic lanes, and introduction of turning lanes have in many ways influenced the image of the public right-of-way, but it will be designed and developed by many designers and decision-makers. The urban designer can exert control over some of the decisions that are made and less control over others. No urban design team can 'design' the whole of Hennepin Avenue in the architectural sense. The urban design task is to understand the system of linkages and interactions within the diverse whole and between it and the rest of the city; to design parts of it; and to help guide and channel the parts

designed by others in a direction beneficial to the city. This task is orchestration as much as design. It is not 'total design', except in the sense of finding a higher order, an organised complexity, within the seeming randomness of the city.

A certain design challenge of the study has been to find an order within the seeming disorder of the Hennepin Avenue environment, a framework within which the variety will appear complex and not ugly. A first approach to such a task is to view Hennepin Avenue in the broader context of Nicollet Mall and other large scale, recent projects in Downtown Minneapolis. In this context, the turbulence of Hennepin Avenue can be seen as a contrast to and a relief from the shining new order around it. As the expanding downtown economy presses for change on Hennepin Avenue, so this difference in identity must be preserved, even as structures are renovated or redeveloped and the Avenue is more intensely used. The entertainment uses, diversity of uses, bright lights, neon lights, will not remain unless they are encouraged. The pressure will be to exchange the red silk petticoat image of Hennepin Avenue for a grey flannel one. Although a grey flannel image may be suitable to, and a valid requirement of, new office and hotel complexes on Hennepin Avenue, this image on the Avenue as a whole would not benefit the city at large. A way must be found to accommodate the bright-lights, entertainment image of the whole, as well as the 'non-commercial' entrance lobbies and approaches needed by new corporate structures on the Avenue.

The urban design plan must accommodate just such relations and potential conflicts. The many and complex interactions that exist between public and private entities on any street can be used to create an urban design strategy for Hennepin Avenue. Public improvements within the right-of-way can provide encouragement to private development and rehabilitation of adjacent properties. The public investment serves as an earnest of the good intentions of the city and provides support for investment from the private sector. The urban design plan can exert considerable design authority over the public sector, the design team can in fact design the public improvements. The plan can influence private sector designs in numerous ways, but it cannot exert total design control over private sector projects. In aesthetic terms, the public improvements can form part of the visual framework that is needed to bring order to the environment. However, on Hennepin Avenue, this ordering effect should be imaginatively applied. Public improvements should be sturdy and scaled to urban mass use (not to campus or neighbourhood-scale use), but they should also be light-in-heart, tuned to the entertainment and recreation atmosphere that is intended for the Avenue. They must be urbane as well as urban.

The aim then, is to produce a design for public improvements in the right-of-way that will help set the tone and image of the Transit-Entertainment Centrum and form a suitable framework for the larger private sector investment that is expected to follow.

Reflector Trees

A most important consideration in supporting the entertainment image was lighting. Careful attention was paid to the variety of atmospheres that can be suggested by street and transit lighting and to the relation of this lighting to private sector light sources in store windows and signs.

Of all the elements available to define the image of the public sector, lighting is the most all-pervading and can be the most magical. More than the other elements of the street furniture or paving, it can define the entertainment ethos of the Avenue. Out of this realisation rose the idea of the 'reflector trees' that are the main form and image givers in the new right of way. These decorations form a continuous lining to the Avenue. Although they span the street in one direction, they are thin in the other

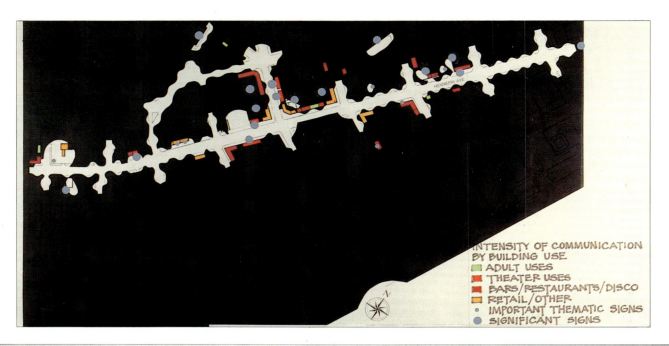

INTENSITY OF COMMUNICATION
BY BUILDING USE
- ADULT USES
- THEATER USES
- BARS/RESTAURANTS/DISCO
- RETAIL/OTHER
- IMPORTANT THEMATIC SIGNS
- SIGNIFICANT SIGNS

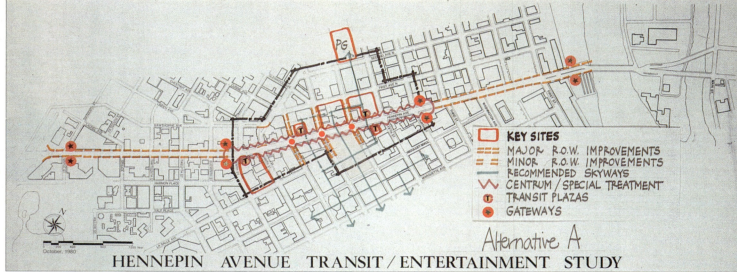

KEY SITES
MAJOR R.O.W. IMPROVEMENTS
MINOR R.O.W. IMPROVEMENTS
RECOMMENDED SKYWAYS
CENTRUM / SPECIAL TREATMENT
T TRANSIT PLAZAS
GATEWAYS

Alternative A

HENNEPIN AVENUE TRANSIT / ENTERTAINMENT STUDY

TRANSIT / ENTERTAINMENT STUDY *ABOVE*: ILLUMINATION AND SIGNS; *BELOW* : IMPROVEMENT PROPOSALS

direction to avoid obstructing the store windows and signs on Hennepin Avenue. They are relatively high to avoid being soiled by the traffic that passes beneath them. Seen from the street at night, the supports will recede from view and the bright white reflectors will appear to dance unsupported across the street to merge with those on the other side. From the sidewalk, the shape of the tree has been carefully disciplined so as not to suggest overhanging branches.

The 'reflector trees' are made of metal. The sparkle elements are coated metal reflectors. They are illuminated by a strong light source in the tree trunk, which acts like a torchere, throwing light upward into the branches. The reflectors seem to attach randomly to the branch structure but are actually carefully spaced to avoid overlapping and to ensure that they will reflect. The lighting source is a long-life, standard metal halide lamp. Its bright white light will distinguish the public sector lighting from the coloured lights and signs of the private sector. The metal tree structure is itself highly decorative. During the day, the fan-like silhouettes of the trees and the delicate tracery of their branches will provide a different experience of the Avenue from the one at night. Tree trunks and branches will be coloured to be in

chromatic contrast with the buildings on Hennepin Avenue. The reflectors are, of course, white.

Sidewalks and Ambience

The sidewalks should enhance the image of urbane sophistication that an entertainment centrum should purvey. Hennepin Avenue is not the main street of a rural eastern town, nor is it a part of colonial Philadelphia. The warm, mellow, textured, uneven appearance of red-brown brick, that is suited to these other locations, would be out of place here. Something smoother, more hard-edged, and more stone-like is indicated, something urbane, which although not mellow, is not unfriendly. Most important, the edge between traffic and people, between street and sidewalk, should be clearly and cleanly marked. This strong edge, well defined, will make pedestrians feel happy and safe on the sidewalk.

On the sidewalks and in the transit plazas alongside Hennepin Avenue, street lamps, benches, and trash cans, must be associated with kiosks, sculptures, decorations and exhibits, as well as with fire hydrants, traffic lights and street signs; all must come together to help maintain the desired image of the Transit/

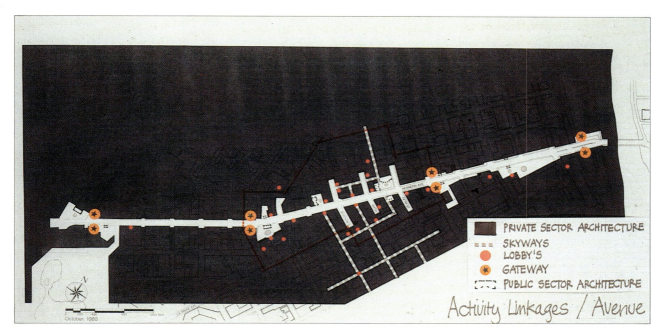

Activity Linkages / Avenue

Legend:
- ■ PRIVATE SECTOR ARCHITECTURE
- ═ ═ SKYWAYS
- ● LOBBY'S
- ✶ GATEWAY
- ⁝ ⁝ PUBLIC SECTOR ARCHITECTURE

October, 1980

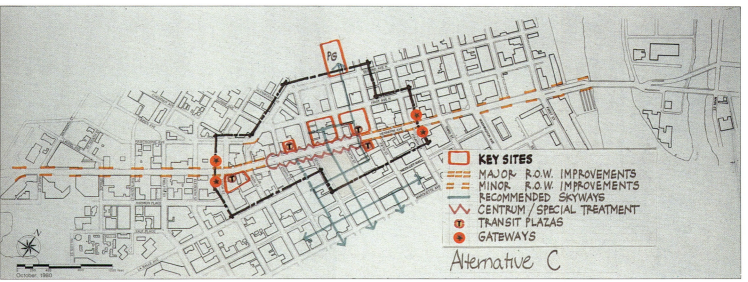

Alternative C

Legend:
- ▢ KEY SITES
- ═ ═ MAJOR R.O.W. IMPROVEMENTS
- ─ ─ MINOR R.O.W. IMPROVEMENTS
- ──── RECOMMENDED SKYWAYS
- ∿ CENTRUM/SPECIAL TREATMENT
- Ⓣ TRANSIT PLAZAS
- ✶ GATEWAYS

October, 1980

TRANSIT / ENTERTAINMENT STUDY, *ABOVE*: ACTIVITY LINKAGES; *BELOW*: IMPROVEMENT PROPOSALS

Entertainment Centrum, night and day, but especially by day when they will be most used. These elements must be tough, sturdy and usable. They must suggest civic scale as well as the elegant sophistication of a bright-light district. They should be grouped together to save space, reinforce the sense of scale, and avoid a spotty, disconnected appearance.

Transit Stations

The major contribution made by transit to the imagery of the Transit/Entertainment Centrum is four transit station buildings, three of which are associated with outdoor plazas. The buildings give weather protection as well as information to crowds waiting at the most heavily used stops on the Avenue. Although the primary use of the transit buildings and plazas is for weather protection for riders, they are planned for various other civic uses as well. And each is intended to serve and enhance the activities and structures in the block or sub-area of Hennepin Avenue where it occurs.

Considerable historic precedent exists in cities such as London, Paris and Vienna, for the design of small transit buildings that are civic works of art. A modern idiom is yet to be found for

such a modest civic amenity, that relates it to the bright lights of an entertainment district and allows it to be visible among the neon without losing its dignity or the possibility of quietness and regeneration that its plaza provides. Transit stations can become key locations for cultural and artistic activities that support the arts and entertainment themes of Hennepin Avenue.

The outdoor plazas are of different sizes and shapes to suit their locations, functions, and the uses they adjoin. However, they are all paved and treed. The tree canopy is set directly beside the right-of-way to hold the building line of the Avenue. At the same time, the trees stand in contrast to the continuous facades of the Avenue as well as to the fantasy trees of the Transit/Entertainment Centrum. In these quiet plazas, trees, furniture groupings, pedestrian lamps, and carefully selected sculptures and art works, will suggest relief from the glitter and sparkle of the street.

Skyways

Although the skyways envisioned by the plan are private constructions, their image is all-important to the public because they cross Hennepin Avenue and are highly visible. Crossing a public

LOCATOR PLAN

SYMBOL KEY

FURNITURE GROUP A (IN TRANSIT STATION ONLY)	■	FURNITURE GROUP B	▲	REFLECTOR TREE	—
FURNITURE GROUP A1	▬	FURNITURE GROUP C	●	GATEWAY	—G
FURNITURE GROUP A2	—	PEDESTRIAN LIGHTS	+	TRANSIT BUILDING	■

ABOVE: PRECEDENT PROPOSALS FOR TRANSIT SHELTERS: *CENTRE*: SECTION THROUGH HENNEPIN AVENUE; *BELOW*: LOCATOR MAP FOR TRANSIT SHELTERS

street should be regarded as a privilege. It is not a right normally conferred by property ownership. In Minneapolis, the granting of this privilege has resulted in benefit to building owners, tenants, and the public. Many are served by the skyway system. However, with the privilege comes responsibility to effect the crossing in a suitable and civic way. What this means for Hennepin Avenue may be quite different from what it means for other parts of the City. Therefore, guidelines should be enforced for skyway design for Hennepin Avenue.

Although they are not at the extremities of the entertainment Centrum, the skyways will be seen as gateways because they span the Avenue. And indeed, because they are important links in a pedestrian network, they do form pedestrian gateways to the Avenue.

Public and Private Plans

The success of plans for the revival of Hennepin Avenue will depend on an active partnership between the public and the private sectors. The public sector primes the pump, gives guidance, offers incentives, and exerts suasion, using all the tools of government available for the purpose. The private sector reacts, responds, rehabilitates, redevelops, and as consumers, votes its support or criticism with its feet.

For this system of action and reaction to succeed, for one governmental dollar to lever seven to ten private dollars, there must be a realistic assessment on the part of government not only of what the City needs from Hennepin Avenue, but also of what those who fulfil the need can provide. It is upon this realistic assessment that a public vision must be built; the vision should be initiated by government and responded to by the private sector creatively. The vision should cover public and private investments, activities and designs.

The plan for Hennepin Avenue is part of that public vision. As such, it delineates both the public sector image and the private sector image, although it contains quite different prescriptions for how to achieve each. Public sector improvements will be built by governmental agencies; those in the private sector by many different groups and individuals, over a much longer time period, although some of these will happen surprisingly quickly.

Basic to the image developed for Hennepin Avenue are the assumptions for intense transit and retail uses, for an entertainment focus, for rehabilitation and redevelopment in office, hotel, and possibly some residential condominium use, and for a prevailing theme of entertainment and bright lights rather than grey flannel respectability.

In this context, a public sector image of bright white lights, 'reflector trees' that define the Avenue, friendly, but muted and civic paving and street furniture, and quiet transportation amenities on a modest scale, is expected to be a foil to something colourful and vital in the private sector. Coloured neon signs should dance down the sidewalk beside the 'reflector trees', crossing over the Avenue at the skyways to join the neon of the opposite sidewalk. Brightly lit store window displays should run the length of the Centrum providing visual interest at ground level and safe, warm light to assure night use of the Avenue.

Existing Buildings

The Hennepin Centre for the Arts, the Lumber Exchange, and Butler Square are excellent examples of how the exteriors of fine Victorian structures can be restored to provide a foil and anchor for everything else that happens by way of regeneration on and near Hennepin Avenue. These do not provide illumination on how to deal with the lesser structures of the Avenue. General design recommendations for such structures and combinations of structures are hard to make, compared with recommendations for, say, the paint-up and fix-up of a Colonial or 19th-century

warehouse street. This is because the styles and types of buildings are so different, one from the other.

New Buildings

There is the possibility of new buildings on Hennepin Avenue, either through infilling or through development of whole blocks or portions of blocks. Infill buildings should derive their character from those around them and be subject to the same guidelines as for existing buildings, more or less. For the new large developments that can or should be encouraged in the Centrum, some general guidelines can be laid down. These new buildings should, in general, maintain the bright lights and retail continuity of street level Hennepin Avenue, but above the ground floor they should act as a foil to both the neon lights and the existing buildings, major and minor, on the Avenue. To do this, they should be suave buildings, in muted colours, grey or bronze, of smooth and precise materials, steel, glass, or polished stone, that present a 'high tech' appearance. The dark, precise, hard-edged quality of these materials will offset as well, the white sparkle and glitter of the entertainment-theme public improvements.

There should be no objection to slab or tower buildings rising from Hennepin Avenue, however, these should be associated with some sort of podium that lines the Avenue and maintains a height of about six or seven stories. Podium and tower should look alike, but the podium walls could be the location for colourful neon signs.

Skyways entering new structures present yet another problem in architectural relations. Architects of new buildings on Hennepin Avenue should be presented with the challenge of the multiple relations each building must observe in both horizontal and vertical directions. It is characteristic of good urban architecture that it has not one, but many images and not one, but many layers of meaning. These new buildings will read from far among the growing number of graceful towers on the central Minneapolis skyline. They will stand as a quiet foil to the entertainment hype of the street although at close quarters, their identity will be lost as they become part of a series of entertaining excitements along the sidewalk.

Implementation

A wide range of methods of achieving aesthetic intentions is available. Various methods are embodied in the mechanisms the City now uses to achieve the general purposes of planning and building. The many design intentions, public and private, of this plan should be related to those existing mechanisms, and if necessary, new methods should be introduced where they are lacking. The aim, however, should be the lightest not the heaviest of controls.

Extract from Urban Design Plan; Hennepin Avenue Transit/Entertainment Study, *City of Minneapolis, 1981.*

Hennepin Avenue Plan (1980-81) Minneapolis, NN; *In collaboration with*: Bennett-Ringrose-Wolsfeld-Jarvis-Gardner, Inc. and Williams/O'Brien Associates, Inc; *In charge*: Denise Scott Brown; *Project Manager*: James H. Timberlake; *With*: Steen Izenour, Steen Kieran, Paul Muller, David Quigley, John Rauch, Miles Ritter, Jeffrey D. Ryan, David Aughan, Robert Venturi

ABOVE: WASHINGTON AVENUE, TYPICAL SECTION; *CENTRE*: SIGNAGE; *BELOW*: GATEWAY BANNER

WASHINGTON AVENUE
Miami Beach

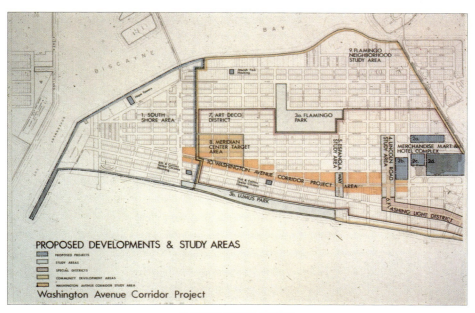

MAP OF CORRIDOR PROJECT

World holiday lore, derived from legends of the rich and famous, embroidered by Hollywood, and re-habilitated by The Late Late Show, places Miami Beach, with Acapulco, the Riveria, Rio, Monte Carlo and Las Vegas in a timeless world of glitter and romance. Young adults of today have their

parents' memories of Miami Beach. Hollywood and Miami Beach – image of exotic palms, the tropics, a large, yellow moon and dark, starry sky as backdrop for the silhouette of two more beautiful than beautiful lovers – these recall, more than any other places, a lyric moment in America's past that still holds fascination for the present.

Flamingoes on the lawns of suburban houses throughout the country attest to the hold of Miami upon the American imagination. Nostalgia for the beautiful past, as it develops in the America of the 1970s, may give tourists and convention goers an added incentive for visiting Miami Beach; to experience a piece of that past that was vivid to them in childhood. This city represents the silver side of the Depression – jazz and the glamour and romance of the films of that era; then, in the 40s, swing, the big bands, Fred Astaire and Ginger Rogers stepping lightly through a world where problems dissolved. Post-War, a trip to Miami Beach still meant removal into a sun-filled life where Hollywood visions of the 30s defined the meaning of luxury. The silver-screen picture does not tarnish although the island may be subject to the vicissitudes of the everyday world.

On the other hand, Miami Beach is not just another urban area in Dade County. Land and buildings for improvement and renewal within the tourist area on the beach, hold an allure that could never be matched by equivalent locations in Miami or even

other coastal resorts. Miami Beach's competitors are international – European, Latin American or Caribbean. However, shifting tides in the international resort and recreation industry, including rising European prices and the devaluation of the dollar, are sharply reordering the competitive advantages of international resort areas. For both modest and luxurious accommodations, Miami Beach may offer Europeans a lower cost vacation than its equivalent at Nice or Cannes, including the air fare. And for habitues of European resorts Miami Beach has the added attraction of novelty. (Paradoxically if European resort trade were to be diverted in noticeable measure to Miami Beach, this might redirect national and local markets toward the City – Americans would come for the European chic.) Miami Beach is a city of all America's groups – of elderly Jewish and younger Cuban communities, even of Cuban Sephardic Jews – living together in the agonised here and now of the Eastern Seaboard in the 1970s, facing its ontological crisis far from the glitter.

Today in Miami Beach, a large, eager and active group works to support significant Beach architecture and urbanism, particularly of the Art Deco and Mediteranean styles, and, as a result, the Miami Beach Architectural District is on the National Register of Historic Places. There is considerable agreement now that the Art Deco buildings of Miami Beach are a priceless heritage of the early 1930s, the more valuable because they occur together in a precinct, which makes them extremely rare in world

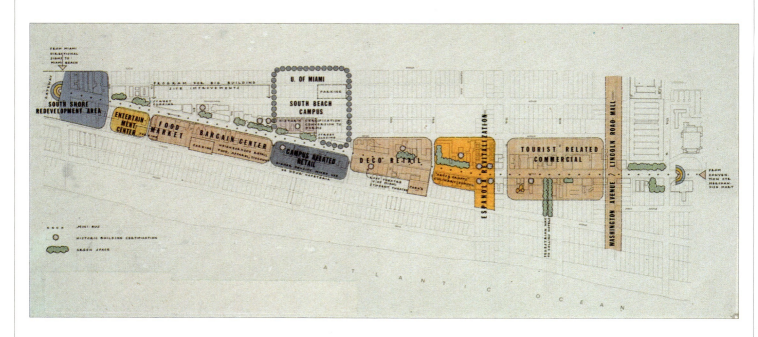

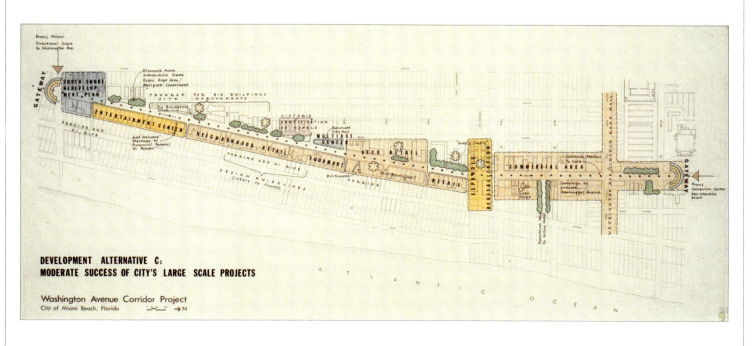

DEVELOPMENT ALTERNATIVE C:
MODERATE SUCCESS OF CITY'S LARGE SCALE PROJECTS

Washington Avenue Corridor Project
City of Miami Beach, Florida

ABOVE: WASHINGTON AVENUE, IMPROVEMENT PROPOSALS: *ABOVE:* DEVELOPMENT PROPOSAL C

ABOVE L TO R: HOTEL ALDEN, BEACON HOTEL; *CENTRE L TO R:* THE BERKLEY SHORE, EUCLID HOTEL; *BELOW L TO R:* BUTCHERS SHOP, CUBANACAN SUPERMARKET

architecture. There are a few such Art Deco precincts in Europe and Africa and almost none in America. A 'Deco District' in Miami Beach will contribute its own unique and not inconsiderable part to the economic revitalisation of the island, especially if judiciously integrated into the marketing strategy for the Beach as a whole. Resorts, because they serve peoples' free-choice, leisure activities, tend to suffer more than other places from fluctuations in taste. Although the lavish hotels and grand scale entertainment that were fashionable in the economic boom period of the 50s and 60s are still popular with many vacationers, a new market has developed nationwide in the 1970s for the small, the preserved, the nostalgic, the natural. The Beach could, very likely, substantially enlarge its tourist pool by using the Deco District in the same way as the Gaslight District is used in St Louis and the Vieux Carré in New Orleans.

Returning the Deco District to itself and making its historic and architectural value apparent will, in turn, throw new light on the later hotels to the north; it will help people rediscover the fabulous. The Deco District will again pull its weight economically for the island, taking part in the continuous creation and recreation of Miami Beach as a holiday paradise.

Washington Avenue is pivotally located in relation to the forces and trends of the 1970s. It is a major north-south arterial of the Beach. Although it has deteriorated into a seedy street of discount stores and cheap restaurants, off it lies the Deco heartland. Here, the creativity of about six architects adopted a style that had been the French, Beaux-Arts-trained architects' reaction to cubism. Adding their own flourishes to suite climate and context, they produced eye-brows, portholes, fleches, boomerangs, flamingos, sunbursts, palm trees, corner windows and streamlined shape – with a verve and sureness that seemed to elude the more respectable architects of the era. As the main street of the Deco District, Washington Avenue is an important commercial strip that serves the shopping needs of local residents and of shoppers for ethnic provisions, island-wide. Physically, it links two outstanding redevelopment projects of the decade, the Civic and Convention Center and the South Shore development. The fate of Washington Avenue is tied to these developments; it will change as they change. The avenue and its adjacent areas will probably assume a major role in accommodating households and establishments relocated as a result of clearance for the South Shore redevelopment. In addition, the symbiosis that exists now between commercial uses on the corridor and residential uses that surround it in the Deco District, will continue for the future. Change in one will bring about change in the other.

A series of questions must be taken into consideration in planning and designing for the future of the corridor: What should be the nature of the interface between Washington Avenue and the large-scale developments, proposed to the north and south of the Deco District? How can existing business activity along Washington Avenue be upgraded to attract more tourists and shoppers? What measures can be adopted to reduce conflict between heavy pedestrian traffic and vehicular traffic?

Aesthetic guidelines for rehabilitation should be a lively reaction to present urban functions and enjoyments and should incorporate a loving respect for the heritage of Washington Avenue. These guidelines should not impose so much control as to stifle innovation (for example, by precluding a possible disco-

théque for the Cinema Theatre) nor should they enforce all-encompassing systems (for exmple, identical awnings of similar colour) that homogenise Washington Avenue's diversity. The guidelines should take a situationist approach that capitalises upon the individuality of Washington Avenue's sub-areas and structures and on the heterogeneity of its activities.

The plan recommends sensitive preservation around Washington Avenue, aimed at enhancing the essence of Miami Beach's nostalgic image: whilst at the same time improving the city's position as an international tourist resort with a stunning, natural geographical location and climate, a varied population, and a range of accommodation from luxury hotels to modest rooms.

The plan tried to reckon with the impact on Washington Avenue of international tourism and of the considerable private sector development taking place north and south of our area, yet to maintain Washington Avenue for its present users and help merchants derive benefit from, rather than be uprooted by, the large-scale changes around them.

The physical recommendations for Washington Avenue arise from recognising its positive aspects – its human scale, its interesting variety of stores, its architecturally important buildings, its position in the Deco District, and the opportunities for improved landscaping – and its negative aspects – the economically marginal character of a significant number of stores and dearth of pedestrian amenities.

To improve the public sector of Washington Avenue, we recommend planting palms and shade trees along the sidewalk. We try to ensure that the tree trunks will be high enough to avoid blocking store windows or obscuring signs. We recommend repaving sidewalks in the tinted pink cement that is traditional on the Beach. Median strips down the centre of the avenue are, we feel, more suited than the sidewalks to contain the lush, exotic landscaping that recall the Hollywood image of Miami Beach.

For the private sector, we have evolved design guidelines tuned to the financial abilities of local merchants. The guidelines discussed colours of masonry and trim, store window decoration and signing, public and private. We recommend paint-up and fix-up of existing Deco facades using light, neutral tones for stucco walls, and for the trim, a 1930s palette of cool, tropical colours. Where the decoration is damaged beyond repair, we recommended repainting with elaborate store signs. Worn-out awnings should be replaced with new ones, preferably canvas, with broad stripes. We set a minimum height for awnings but no other constraints. One excellent way of achieving aesthetic excellence is to employ excellent designers.

Extracts from City of Miami Beach, Washington Avenue Revitalisation Plan, *for the City of Miami Beach Planning Department, 1979*

Venturi and Rauch, *Partner-in-Charge*: Denise Scott Brown; *Project Director*: Mary Yee; *Senior Planner*: James Allen Schmidt; *Architect*: Fredric Schwartz; *Landscape Architect*: Frances Hundt; *With the assistance of*: Thomas Bernard, David Brisbin, Janet Colesberry, Mark Hewitt, Steven Izenour, Steven Kieran, Christine Matheu, David Marohn, Paul Muller, James Timberlake, Robert Venturi; *Associate Architect*: David Jay Feinberg AIA, Architect, P.A.; *With the assistance of*: Marcia Esquenazi; *Consulting Architect*: Richard Rose, Architect; *With the asistance of*: Susi Ronai, Hugh Kerr

*

ANCIENT MEMPHIS ON THE NILE

MODERN MEMPHIS ON THE MISSISSIPPI

PEABODY PLACE & BEALE STREET
Downtown Memphis

MEMPHIS, AERIAL VIEW

For Memphis, the Mississippi has been an incessant problem and opportunity. It has challenged Memphians to think strategically, because life and livelihood have depended on the ability to use its resources. Citizens of river cities learn to be canny. When the cotton market declined in the mid-South, some Memphis merchants and factors adapted their warehouses and marketing to the new

crops in the region. Others concentrated on industries related to cotton and built up Memphis as a service and information centre to the cotton industry. Yet others marketed their real estate and became developers; while some followed the shifting cotton market where it led them, to Texas and later the Far East. They went down the Mississippi to join the world economy.

Artistic movements paralleled the flow of cotton and the river. The blues and rock were country musics that followed trade routes to the city. They achieved their identity in Memphis then flowed down the river and over the airwaves, taking Memphis with them to the world.

Memphis's unique location on the Mississippi established the city's earliest economic strategies and its first plan: it still holds the key to development today. Today, economic advantage derives more from the amenity of river, bluffs and view than from river-based industry. Economic linkage between town and wharf continues, but greater value now resides in the historical importance, symbolism and beauty of the connection.

The pattern engendered by the earliest relation between resources, transportation routes, and settlement still forms the basic stress diagram of Memphis. Over the years, pressures on this diagram have altered with changes in the economy, technology and social life, and the pattern has been intensified, overlaid or obscured as the relative weights of its elements altered.

A main tenet of the plan is that it begin with the historical link

between Memphis and the Mississippi river and with an understanding of the urban pattern this connection has induced. Policies should be sought that clarify the basic relationships, using them to produce urban amenities that will help preserve economic viability.

As the flow of the Nile determined the economy of ancient Egypt, so the Mississippi was the moving force in the development of the mid-South. Each river gave birth and form to its Memphis. Some historical forces were favourable – the advent of steam and rail – and others catastrophic – destruction through earthquakes and near obliteration through yellow fever.

The 1950s saw the initiation of a long period of decline as citizens turned toward the suburbs. After the death of Dr Martin Luther King Jr, the trend accelerated. The marks of citizen and government reaction to Center City decline are immediately with us: physical deterioration, then attempts to rectify it through federally aided projects to attract Memphians back to the city. Mid-America Mall, the Conference Center, the Civic Center, Beale Street renewal, and the Mud Island complex are such attempts. They have met with mixed success. Some private development – the Peabody Hotel and the Morgan Keegan building – has been successful; yet neither public nor private projects have been assimilated into the urban pattern, and the areas of clearance that surround them resemble a wasteland.

In the early 1980s a spurt of building suggested that the

MEMPHIS AND SHELBY COUNTY

balance of Center City might be altered once again. Memphians feared that the new infusions could be as disjointed and disparate as earlier renewal efforts had been and that they would obscure the existing pattern without rendering a clear new pattern. To maintain the advantage of its good situation, Center City needed a strategic overview of its future development, and policies and guidelines to help public and private actors on the Center City stage to understand their individual and group decisions in the light of the whole. This was the reason for the commissioning of the Center City Development Plan.

The Development Plan

Center City is primarily a work place that draws residents of communities to it. It contains facilities that are unique to the region, and it faces unique problems different from those of suburban communities. Because the Center City-medical center combination forms the hub of the regional transportation system, changes downtown affect movement patterns beyond its borders, and changes within the regional transportation network are of vital importance to downtown. In addition, Center City has more of the conditions that call for planning – more density, more

congestion, more traffic, more land use types, more economic linkages, and more stakeholders with legitimate interests in its success. The plan for center city should, therefore, be different in both degree and type from plans for residential communities. It must be more broadly based, strategic and interdisciplinary; a greater involvement in its making is required of all the agencies of government, to meet concerns that range from regional transportation to specialised education. Its needs are so demanding that the agency that plans for it should have Center City as its prime focus.

The Center City Development Plan is a strategy plan. The mandate given the consultant team was to produce an overview of Center City Memphis and its key issues and to suggest general directions that policies should take over the next 25 years to nurture downtown's heritage and guide its growth. Our approach was to be interdisciplinary. Our recommendations were to be visionary, but only as that word can apply in urban America today – that is, they were to lie at the optimistic end of the feasibility range.

The plan addresses three basic necessities:
1. The need for Center City to achieve its full potential and to

MEMPHIS' CITIZENS HIDING COTTON AND SUGAR DURING THE CIVIL WAR

play an important role in the regional economy.

2. There should be a clear urban design concept for Center City, one that will build on the beauty of its location and its long history, uniting old and new into a vital image for the whole.

3. The plan must maintain a balance between preservation of the past and the development of new initiatives. Downtown has many fine old buildings that give special ambience to the area. Its historic and spectacular relationship to the river and its history-laden patterns of streets and open spaces are part of the fabric to be preserved and restored, for economic as well as aesthetic reasons.

Obviously, a strategy plan is not a complete blueprint for action. Its recommendations for the short run may be quite specific while those for the medium and long range will require detailed development in the future, when they come in line for implementation. Planning must provide answers to short-term questions, as well as thoughtful guidelines for long-term policies and commitments. There was recognition that innovative and imaginative urban design, although important, would not be sufficient to produce a useful plan, and that analytic talent and integrative imagination were required in all fields, from develop-

ment economics to the study of inner-city populations.

The Development Strategy

At the end of the analysis and goal formulations tasks, the process of moving from goals to policies began, with a consideration of alternative ways of meeting goals. Alternative economic scenarios, transportation plans and growth patterns were considered, and the Policy Committee was asked to choose among them, once the implications of each had been spelled out. With choices made, the Planning Team was faced with the task of conforming the choices to each other to produce a co-ordinated development strategy.

The first-draft land use plan which resulted foresaw the achievement of development intentions both north and south; around the Convention Center to the north and at Peabody Place, Beatle Street and Orpheum Plaza Towers to the south. These areas of new development would frame the old core and, by channeling growth to its edges, help to protect it. In the core, a rehabilitated Mid-America Mall and a re-established set of connections to the riverside and across the Wolf River to Mud Island would stimulate preservation and rehabilitation.

ABOVE L TO R: ELVIS PRESLEY, MEMPHIS PROPOSAL ILLUSTRATION; *CENTRE L TO R:* PEABODY PLACE, BEALE STREET; *BELOW:* VIEWS OF THE MISSISSIPPI RIVER

ABOVE L TO R. POSTCARD OF MEMPHIS. W C HARDY; *CENTRE L TO R*: BEALE STREET BY NIGHT& BY DAY; *BELOW L TO R*: MEMPHIS FROM THE RIVER. THE MISSISSIPPI FROM MEMPHIS

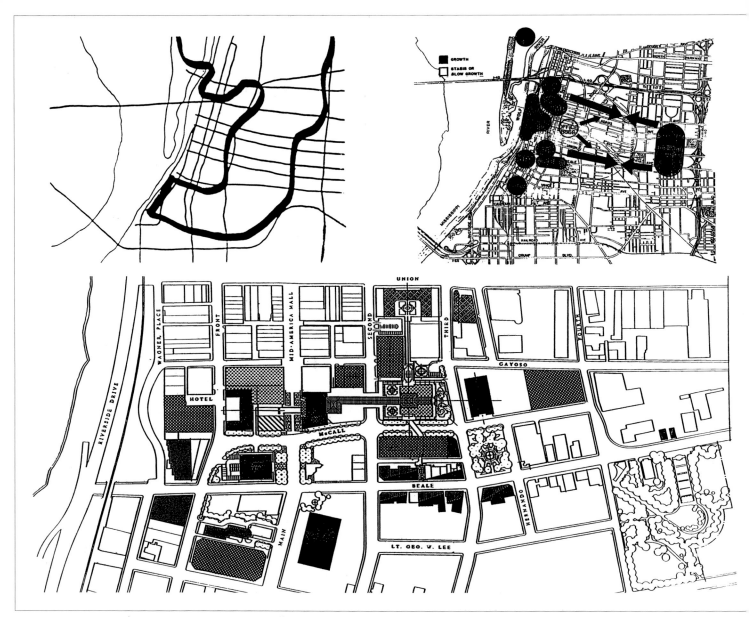

ABOVE L TO R: DIAGRAM OF INNER CITY HOUSING, DEVELOPMENT INTENTIONS ACHIEVED; BELOW: LAND USE PLAN

A transportation plan that introduced no new expressways, but upgraded existing facilities, would help reinforce the development aim, by maintaining the relationship between the core and Riverside Drive and by channeling future growth eastward along existing arterials such as Union and Poplar Avenues.

The Urban Design Plan

The urban designer has been compared to the conductor of an orchestra or to a painter who attempts to paint a picture on a river. Urban designers must proceed in tandem with decisions on city-wide relationships and on street lights, and with choices whose impacts will be known tomorrow and the next century. A clear urban design concept for Center City should unite individual projects into an overall image. It must embrace a wide spectrum of design levels, from large-scale, city-wide relationships and the overall character and texture of the city, to small-scale details of street fronts, sidewalks, and signage.

In the early phases of the study of Memphis we analysed many aspects of downtown and its surrounding neighbourhoods, including land uses, streets, parks, rivers, civic and community facilities, and monuments and symbols. We described the func-

tional relationships and economic linkages that exist between the physical components of center city; for example, between buildings and sidewalks, public and private spaces, buildings and parks, parking and roads, the river and the river edge. We discussed the architectural character of important building groupings around Court Square, Mid-America Mall, and the Civic and Justice Centers, alongside Riverside Drive, and on Beale Street. We surveyed key buildings and spaces, important institutions, monuments, views and vistas, and unique streets and buildings.

Owing to the unique location of downtown Memphis, urban design has been assigned considerable importance in the Center City Development Plan. A major reason for commissioning the plan was fear that development could compromise the economic viability of downtown by destroying its beauty and amenity.

The mission of the urban design plan is to help Center City become the best of its self and to offer its own essence symbolically, culturally, and perhaps morally, to the region and the world. Only in this way can downtown compete with suburban centres and pull its weight in the city.

Center City's main urban design opportunities lie in the fact that it has an absolutely unique location on a river that means so

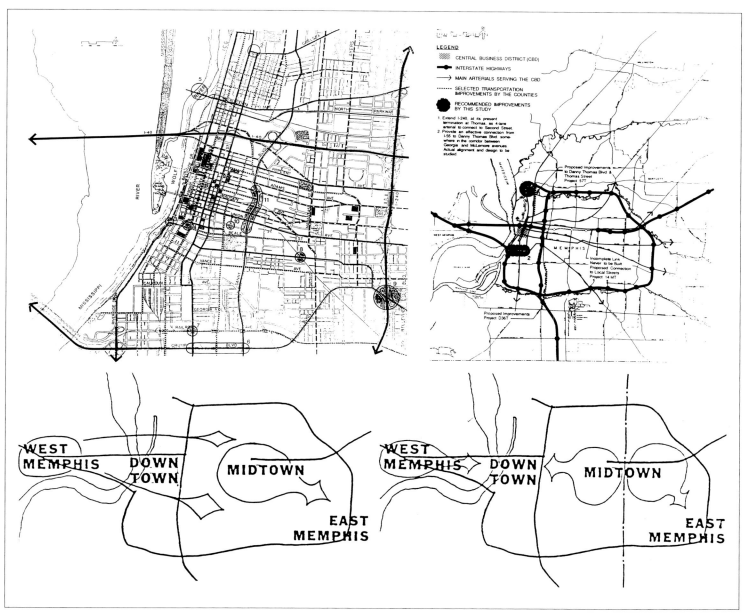

ABOVE: REORIENTATING MIDTOWN TOWARDS DOWNTOWN;*BELOW L* TO *R*: REGIONAL HIGHWAY NETWORK, RECOMMENDED TRANSPORTATION IMPROVEMENTS

much to all Americans, and a potentially excellent relationship between the city and the river; an historic urban grid adaptable for today and well related to the Mississippi and Wolf Rivers; a set of meaningful symbols, derived from Memphis's long history and multiple talents; a walkable and urbane center that contains memorable streetscapes as well as fine examples of architecture, a variety of precincts within and around the centre, which offer anchor points for developments of different kinds; an interesting stock of existing buildings, well suited for conversion to new uses relevant to downtown living; land available for development in different sectors; and a capacity for growth within the existing street and development pattern and the heritage of the historic plan.

Center City's main urban design problems are that it has heritage of projects that have not worked together and have resulted in deterioration, vacancies, closures, and a series of underused, interstitial areas; and development that is strung out and weighted to the north, so that southern portions of downtown have little to support them.

Weaknesses of the Center City physical environment include lack of a 'this is Memphis' feel and look to downtown; loss of the clarity of the very fine 1819 town plan; blocked views of the Mississippi from Front Street; a riverfront that is blighted, ignored, and underused; a riverfront freight line that conflicts with local street traffic, impedes potential development, and prevents pedestrian access to the river; isolated 'spots' of development – Beale Street, the Orpheum, the Peabody, Court Square, the Convention Center – with no 'glue' in between; acres of vacant 'urban renewal' land south and north of Beale Street; a too long, too empty, too bare pedestrian mall; an ill-defined, unattractive Civic Center Square; and a 'no man's land' between downtown and the Medical Center.

Plan for the Beatle Street – Peabody Place Sub-area

This sub-area plan provides an example of how a small-scale historic environment may be related to large new projects, to the advantage of each. Because the Beale Street – Peabody Place sub-area is highly varied, its plans and guidelines cover several types of city centre environments. Therefore its recommendations can serve as models for the development of design guidelines for other sub-areas, both new and historic.

Peabody Place, as a high-quality retail shopping complex, has

AREA SIGNS FOR THE MEMPHIS IMPROVEMENT SCHEME

the potential for creating its own downtown market and for attracting people to come downtown to shop who currently do not do so. The project is sponsored by an established developer, is linked to the very successful Peabody Hotel and already has funding in place. Not only would the project provide a wide range of new downtown jobs and support downtown housing efforts, but such a significant private investment would be a very positive sign to other private developers. Peabody Place would help to establish the type of market conditions necessary to make other projects feasible, most notably the upgrading of stores along Mid-America Mall and the completion of Beale Street.

The original justification of the Beale Street project was a commemoration of the Black cultural-experience and the Memphis music tradition. Over the years this focus has become diluted and the tenanting of Beale Street has been directed towards a more general collection of shops and restaurants. The theme of the Black cultural experience and Memphis music tradition should be strongly re-established as the theme of Beale Street in order to give this project a unique function in the Memphis entertainment and tourist market. A strong commitment to this theme would then be reflected in a reorganisation of

the project as follows: The combination of the rehabilitated Beale Street and Peabody Place, the proposed mixed-use project to span several blocks to the north of Beale Street, should produce a strong anchor for downtown at its southern end, as well as a gateway to residential communities further south. This area is second only to the riverfront in its potential to offer something unique that differentiates downtown from other centers in the region.

The sub-area plan proposes Beale Street's return to its original black musical and cultural theme. It supports the Peabody Place project, which places an upscale, internal, multi-story commercial mall between Mid-America Mall, the Peabody Hotel conference centre and Handy Park, and returns three razed city blocks to the urban fabric.

Two high-rise buildings are recommended as part of Peabody Place. They are important to the urban design plan, but even more important to the goals of absorbing urban growth where there is capacity for it. And they support plans for Beale Street. Their sites should not be pre-empted for less intense uses. Our indicative site plan for Peabody Place may not resemble the final design for that project. However, that design should hold to our

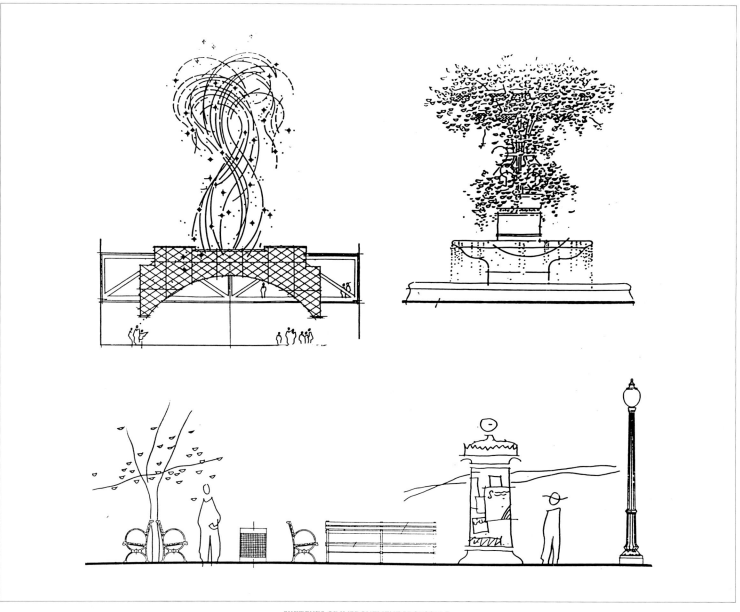

SKETCHES OF IMPROVEMENT PROPOSALS

guidelines, particularly concerning intensity of use and the location of pedestrian access points from Peabody Place Mall to Mid-America Mall, Beale Street and Handy Park.

The old buildings of Beale Street can provide uniqueness and depth to the new of Peabody Place and the new project should help the old establish a present-day identity it has not yet found. Beale Street, standing, at the moment, high and dry in a sea of parking, could be helped to offer its important symbolic and historical contribution to the revitalizing of downtown. Its identity as the historic main street of Memphis's black community, its role in the history of the Blues and the history of the civil rights movement, and its location at the seam between downtown and an important inner-city, black community and an emerging, art-oriented, residential community, suggests that it is a possibility for richness, as well as a meeting place – between black and white, residential and downtown, cultural (the Orpheum and the Peabody Hotel) and commercial (the Mall and Peabody Place). If plans for Peabody Place come to successful fruition, their impact will be to reorient retail activity in the downtown, in both type and location. Peabody Place could attract new downtown growth to the south-eastern quadrant of Center City, forming the point of

origin of a growth front that presses toward the Medical Center along east-west streets.

It is important that the Beale Street – Peabody Place project be planned so as to support existing aims for Beale Street, Mid-America Mall, and the residential communities to the south, as well as to reinforce plans for the network of roads in the region, ingress and egress to department stores, parking, hotel and office lobbies, service bays, and Beale Street stores should be so connected as to reinforce other commercial uses on surrounding streets and particularly on Mid-America Mall and Beale Street. The change in level, east to west across the Peabody Place site, allows for street entrance to the project at several different levels and, therefore, encourages an interesting, multi-level interior.

Community Participation

Center City, in a variety of ways, belongs to all Memphians. Office workers, shoppers, merchants, residents, property owners, restauranteurs, theatre goers, and others from many walks of life and from throughout the metropolitan area have varying stakes in downtown's vitality as the heart of a region, the seat of city and county government, a centre of business, entertainment

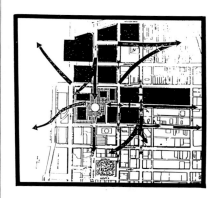
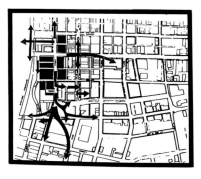

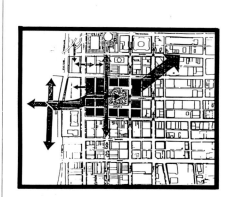
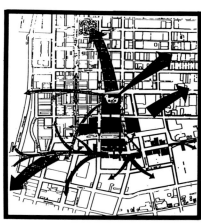

ABOVE: MEMPHIS FROM THE MISSISSIPPI; *CENTRE*: POTENTIAL LINKAGES; *BELOW*: SKETCH OF DEVLEOPMENT CONCEPT FOR MUD ISLAND

and cultural activity, and a link to the founding and growth of Memphis. In addition, elements of a downtown plan are the responsibility of several governmental agencies whose concerns overlap. The constituency for a Downtown plan is, therefore, broad and highly diverse. Reaching its members, soliciting their opinions, informing them, and interacting with them has been an important part of producing the plan. Community participation was achieved through representational democracy (the Policy Committee advised by the Technical Committee), direct democracy (public meetings), community outreach (the media), and interaction of individual community members or groups with the CCC and project team.

The Policy Committee can be an efficient form of community participation if it is representative of all groups who have a stake in, and can veto, the plan. If the mandate to the Committee is not only to guide and advise the planning and implementation process, but also to carry information and progress reports back to their constituencies, this will help to ensure that there are few surprises for the public as implementation proceeds.

The Technical Committee was composed of representatives of agencies whose functions concerned the planning and operating of Center City. The purpose of forming this committee was to provide a body of advice to the Policy Committee in its deliberations on the plan.

The Technical Committee provided a locus for sharing plans and information between the various agencies involved with downtown. In the process the CCC was enabled to establish its presence in decision making on transportation, housing, contiguous communities and other issues of concern to the Center City community.

Public meetings should continue as one means of reaching concerned citizens. Meetings could, in the future, be targeted at specific interest groups – in the arts, commerce, adjacent communities, the educational community – rather than toward an undefined 'public.'

Most people do not go to public meetings. Yet many angry people will attend if the news they hear is an unpleasant surprise. This suggests that the CCC must find ways, apart from convening meetings, to reach people where they are.

While the means for reaching Center City's constituencies are carefully planned and broad-based, there is no substitution for face-to-face meeting. During the study, members of the planning team met with downtown residents, merchants and others, concurrent with other team activity in Memphis. In addition, interviews were held with key individuals and we also-conducted a day-long discussion session where team members and Policy and Technical committee members participated in wrapping up tasks and launching new tasks. This form of interaction is the method of communication the CCC conducts day-to-day. It should easily be expanded to handle ongoing questions of planning, implementation and development.

A powerful means of communicating the goals and plans of Center City with the public, is by making the results of those plans visible to the public. Results could be growth of downtown employment or businesses, increased liveliness on Beale Street, or support for the construction of a high school for the performing arts. Visible signs of progress are perhaps the best communicators. More than Sunday supplements or public meetings, they will provide the evidence people need to make them support the plan by living, working, shopping and recreating downtown.

Conclusion

There is an advantage in having lived a length of time beside the city during the planning process. We have seen several phases of development and, by watching the trends, have learned the complexity of Memphis's opportunities and problems. Time has allowed options and issues of Memphis to be profoundly addressed; this indepth study should give staying power to the plan.

The plan is visionary, but in a realistic way. Its vision is tied to its social and economic aspirations rather than to technological or architectural fantasies – beauty is to be drawn from Center City's physical and social reality (even its hard reality) and from the heritage of its past. The achieving of such a vision requires resourcefulness: methods for its implementation must derive more from Huck Finn's nimble footwork than from the fiat of the pharaohs. If the plan is to guide the development of Center City in a meaningful way, its provisions should be part of a shared information base of Center City's movers and shakers.

Once the plan is approved, the recommended implementation process should be set in motion. Some of the steps are urgent and should be initiated immediately upon approval.

Our hopes for Memphis are that:
– One year from now, everyone in Center City will have heard of the plan, partly because its recommendations are being hotly debated in the context of ongoing development.
– Five years from now, projects will be rising in key locations and the outline of something new and exciting will be visible to everyone.
– Twenty-five years from now, the new city skyline will provide ample evidence, and a symbol, that Memphians can build, socially as well as physically, for now and the future, in the tradition of the best that they have inherited.

Extracts from The Center City Development Plan for Downtown Memphis, *for the Memphis Center City Commission, 1987.*

Consultant Team, Memphis Center City Development Plan. Venturi, Rauch and Scott Brown, Philadelphia, PA, Urban Design and Planning, *Principal in Charge*: Denise Scott Brown; *Project Manager:* Gabrielle London; *With the assistance of*: John Andrews, Eric Van Aukee, Penny Baker, Catherine M Cosentino, Nance Goldenberg, Steve Izenour, James Kolker, Robert Marker, Daniel K McCoubrey, Linda Payne, Beth Rahe, Ivan Sterfan Saleff, Susan Scanlon, R David Schaff; *Economic Development*: Arthur D Little, Inc., Cambridge, MA; *Officer in Charge*: Ronald S Jonash; *With assistance of*: Pam McNamara, John Wehner; *Urban Planning and Transportation Planning*: Killinger Kise Franks Straw, Philadelphia, PA; *Principal in Charge*: James Nelson Kise; *Consultant Principal*: Scott W Killinger; *Project Director*: Massoud Mohadjeri; *With the asaistance of*: D K Jonhston, William Menke, Yao Hwa Tsai; *Traffic Engineer and Transportation Planner*: Robert L Morris, Bethesda, MD; *Minority Consultant*: Reva M Kriegel; *Project Manager*: Grace Cox; *With the assistance of*: Reginald Beal, Jacqueline Horton, Booker Middleton; *Economic Development*: Urban Partners, Philadelphia, PA; *Principal in charge*: John Andrew Gallery; *With the assistance of*: James E Hartling, Peter Lapham; *Preservation, Cultural Planning, and Urban Design*: James Williamson/Carl Awsumb/Architects, Memphis, TN; *Principal in charge*: James F Williamson; *Arts and Cultural Resources*: Pan Awsumb, Consultant; *With the assistance of*: Carl Awsumb, Dan Becker, Cathy Cosentino, Susan Davis, John Runkle

AERIAL VIEW OF AUSTIN

THE REPUBLIC SQUARE DISTRICT
Austin

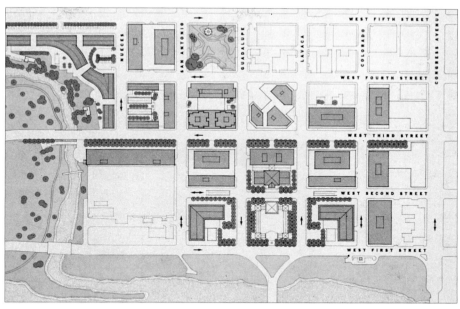

MAP OF AUSTIN

Austin is not on the unending plains, it is not dry and dusty, it does not subscribe to Texas bigness, and it is not Houston. The things that it is not, endear Austin to Texans and intending sun-belt settlers nationwide. The affection is equally flattering and embarrassing; the large numbers of both would be and actual immigrants threaten the maintenance of those very qualities that attract them to Austin.

An aerial view of Austin city centre reveals the original city grid plan: set on Town Lake between two creeks, it is orthogonally organised with reference to topography. The Capitol breaks the grid at the crossing of two important streets, one of which runs south to the lake. In the land between Capitol and river, four quadrants are created by the insertion of four public parks. This plan is familiar to those who know William Penn's original plan for Philadelphia. Like that earlier plan, Austin's has served the city well from its inception and into the automobile age; yet in some ways it has been irrelevant to the growth and dynamic of the city. With the new growth of the 1970s and 1980s, a coarser urban texture has developed as new structures are built on whole blocks or large portions of blocks. The towers of office buildings, defined by their long black shadows, seem almost to stalk across the plan, headed southwest from the Capitol and Congress Avenue toward the old warehouse district that sits between Congress Avenue, Shoal Creek, Sixth Street and Town Lake. This area of low, mostly single-storey, loft structures has a secluded and private air, like an enclave. The aerial photograph suggests that distance from the central core alone did not cause its slow development but also the fact that bridges over Shoal Creek occur at First, Fifth and Sixth Streets only. Limited access made the interior of the southwest sector a quiet, inner pocket.

Although the future of the southwest quadrant seems clearly defined by the trajectory of recent development, projections of that future based on present trends must be mediated by an assessment of the goals, perceptions and actions of Austinites, public and private. A desire to preserve the essence of Austin can be discerned in the zoning regulations that govern height, bulk, type and intensity of use in the CBD, and even more strongly, in the zoning proposals for the Capitol view corridor, overlay zones and historic district. Plans for the creeks and the treatment of the waterfront on either side of Town Lake are other indicators.

The Watson-Casey Companies approached Venturi, Rauch and Scott Brown in May 1983, with the request to help the project team define suitable goals for development within the southwest quadrant. Their question was: Given the inherited structure of the warehouse district, the character of Austin, the projected level and type of demand for land, the constraints of regulations, and the overall aspirations of Austin, is there a good form of new development that can meet pressures, restrictions, aspirations and values, achieve the economic programme and also satisfy the urge to create and celebrate?

Although this was a study for private development, the interplay between public and private sectors was central to the project. In particular, the Laguna Gloria Art Museum's plan to establish a downtown presence on a site donated by the Watson-Casey Companies was considered a key to the initial development of the project. The aim was to define a unified concept for architecture and economics which would result not merely in

SKETCHES SHOWING HEIGHT CONSIDERATIONS FOR AUSTIN

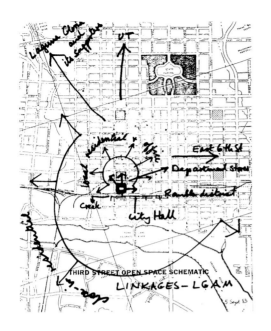

THIRD STREET OPEN SPACE SCHEMATIC
LINKAGES — LGAM

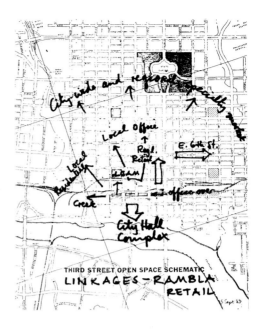

THIRD STREET OPEN SPACE SCHEMATIC
LINKAGES — RAMBLA RETAIL

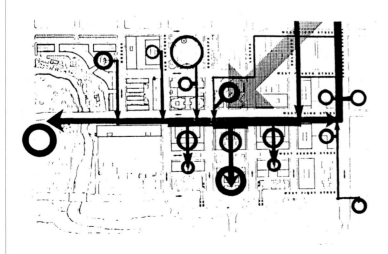

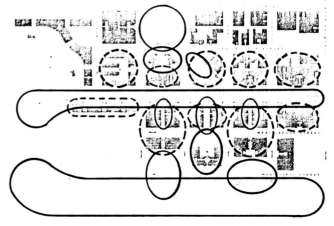

ABOVE: LINKAGE CONSIDERATIONS FOR THE RAMBLA; *CENTRE*: HEIGHT LINE OF CONGRESS AVENUE; *BELOW L* TO *R*: THE RAMBLA'S PEDESTRIAN INFLUENCE. LEVELS OF PRIVACY

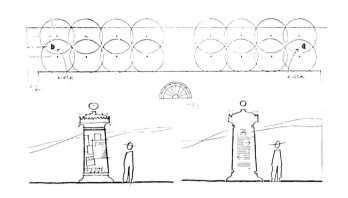

THE AUCTION OAKS

LAVACA

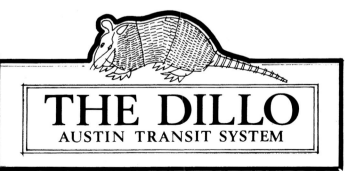

THE DILLO
AUSTIN TRANSIT SYSTEM

ABOVE L TO R: STUDY FOR LANDSCAPE PROPOSAL, VIEW WEST DOWN THE RAMBLA; *CENTRE* AND *BELOW*: AREA SIGNS FOR AUSTIN

good economics or good architecture, but also in a vital city, where public and private, mundane and sublime, buildings and landscape all support each other. Therefore, as much as good design and strategic planning, Austin needed creative suggestions for linkages, between activities proposed for the area and between the new development and existing city.

To undertake this work we made a 'sketchbook' of existing architecture, cityscape and landscape in Austin and analysed how certain long-standing relationships, between, for example, stores and sidewalks, have developed over the years. We calculated the holding capacities of 25 Austin blocks, based on their dimensions, accessibility within the street hierarchy, and zoning controls and other applicable regulations. We considered regional and local economic pressures as they impinged on the area and existing linkages between activities.

A key element of the strategy plan was the proposals for the 'Rambla District'. This name, given to the blocks north and south of Third street from Congress to Shoal Creek, derives from Las Ramblas in Barcelona, a tree-lined pedestrian way at the centre of a series of streets. Always bustling, it is bordered by shops and stalls beside which are zones of theatres, restaurants and hotels as well as other zones of bars, cafes and movie houses.

Like its progenitor, the Austin Rambla is a tree-lined pedestrian avenue located on the railroad right-of-way at the edge of Third Street. We recommend that the Austin version be called 'The Rambla' because it is one street long, not several, and because the mixture of Anglo and Spanish in the name represents the mixture in Austin. On a more abstract level, the change of the name says the Spanish idea is adapted, not merely lifted.

What we have named The Rambla District is intended as the main locus for office and retail activities in the Republic Square District. As such, it requires one overarching theme or identity that will establish it as a most desirable place to be; best achieved by the introduction of an element beyond the office and retail uses, one that could hold its own against the heavy one-way traffic projected for Third Street. The idea of The Rambla was chosen for this purpose. It is a 45 ft wide, tree-lined walk that runs from Congress Avenue to Shoal Creek. It forms the major distributive spine for pedestrian movement coming from the north and south. Pedestrians heading south and west or north and east would be likely to divert to The Rambla as soon as possible to enjoy the shaded walk and the attractive stores alongside.

The Rambla is set to one side of Third Street in order to maintain a pedestrian flow beside retail uses. As Third Street traffic is one way, there is no reason to place the walkway on a median strip. In addition, we have tried to keep The Rambla narrow in order to maintain the linkage between retail fronts on either side of Third street. The Rambla trees should be of moderate height and broad canopy; we prefer the traditional shape of the live oak, but if live oaks would not do well in such a location, perhaps another Texas shade tree could be found.

A prime function of The Rambla will be lunch hour strolling, brown-bagging, sitting, and watching. Even in winter, it should be possible, at mid-day, to sit out on a bench, bundled up warmly, and enjoy the break from heated office space. During the summer, The Rambla, at its hottest, can still provide a respite from the onslaughts of air conditioning. Therefore, between trees there are benches, paired back to back to face into and away from The Rambla. Sidewalk cafes can serve from abutting stores onto The Rambla. Entry points to buildings can be marked by kiosks, statues or fountains. Second and third floor office and retail uses will have a pleasant view of foliage. We would like to see The Rambla installed all at once and early, to be in position before the first office building on the south side opens. The Rambla is a simple facility that will be outstanding through its location, length and use. Although simple in concept, it ties the new

development to the Austin love of outdoors and to the traditional landscape, in a highly urbanistic way; and it will provide a framework that can evoke many ideas for its use. Its evocative quality will contribute to the vitality of the District.

The Rambla should not be a contained and secluded 'Piazza Navona'. It is important for the retail uses on Third Street and for the distributive function and identity of The Rambla that it tie into the fabric of the city by connecting Congress Avenue to Shoal Creek, both points of high pedestrian volume. The Avenue has recent sidewalk and street improvements, and high-rise office and hotel buildings are planned for its southern end. The creek and its trails will attract local workers and residents as well as outdoors lovers city-wide. At Shoal Creek a descent from the Rambla to the water should be planned with an attractive pedestrian destination at the end. At the west end of block 23, a platform looking across the creek, should invite joggers, hikers and bikers to pull in for a rest stop.

Just as we are against the formation of superblocks in most cases but would promote one in the most important civic area, so would we entertain the possibility of skyway links between blocks 20, 21 and 22 without feeling they should be considered elsewhere. These blocks represent the most intense build-up of office and retail uses in the District and their relation to City Hall gives them a semi-public quality. Within the overall plan, they are correctly located and should be kept as compact as possible. The skyway links may provide renting and financing flexibility to meet unknown market contingencies and they will certainly allow indoor access to retail for office tenants. However, they will detract from the vitality of The Rambla. If cross street links are in fact part of the final project, means should be employed to maintain the relation of street level retail to The Rambla, and it becomes doubly important that The Rambla continue to Congress Avenue and Shoal Creek. If the links are not necessary, they should not be built. If built, they should give direct access onto The Rambla. Stairways up from The Rambla at street edge could form abutments to the skyway bridges and could descend to the parking structures below.

For the higher floors of the three Rambla blocks, ingenuity will be needed to achieve the required area of office uses and yet maintain the shape and perimeter desired by high rental customers. We would opt for north-south facing towers, particularly because of the view. The upper floors on block 21 facing the park could be different from and higher than the others. If there is no City Hall park, the three buildings should be equal in height.

The character of The Rambla should be public, civic and sturdy. The interior malls should be civic, semi-public and elegant. The mall through block 21, the central block facing the park, should be larger and more civic than those on either side.

The designs of stores on The Rambla and in the malls should be different from each other. On The Rambla, stores should be light, spacious and inviting through their openness to the sidewalk. Those in the malls should suggest luxury, intensity or the out-of-the ordinary. Elevator lobbies in the malls should be carefully demarcated from retail areas and should express 'grey flannel' aspirations.

The exteriors of buildings on The Rambla should register a similar gradation between private and public. The ground floor of each block should have an auspicious entry point from The Rambla suitable to the prestige of the offices above, but also suggestive of the brightness and bustle of the retail uses in the mall. Signs should be allowed and encouraged on the ground floor facade as a means of maintaining the vitality of The Rambla despite the preponderance of inward-facing retail. The foliage of Rambla trees, desirable though it is, will block the view of store signs. Care should therefore be taken to ensure that Rambla store windows are visible and attractive from across

Third Street. We have recommended that an approximately 40 ft parapet height and setback line be maintained along the length of The Rambla to give scale and human relationship to the project. The setback need not be deep to achieve this effect.

The outer skins of buildings on The Rambla should be suave and self-effacing. Learning from Austin, their refined detailing should be noticed at second glance; no over-insistent texture should draw excessive attention to them. We recommend against cladding these buildings in glass and would like to see a high quality finish of stone veneer or possibly porcelain. The colour choice should take heed of precedent and fall within the range of cream-beige to pale grey. The tops of the office towers on blocks 20, 21 and 22 should form a pleasing silhouette. They will be seen as a backdrop to the new city hall from across Town Lake.

At the northern edge of Third Street, an average-width Austin sidewalk has stores facing onto it from the ground floors of blocks 26, LGAM, 27 and 28. The architecture of this side of Third Street need not be as unified as that of blocks 20, 21 and 22, but it should be urbanely reticent, in keeping with the character that will be established for The Rambla District.

John Reps, writing in 1979, suggested: 'If the buildings of central Austin do not yet match in quality that of the base from which they rise, perhaps time will remedy this shortcoming.' He missed some delights of the architecture of Austin which we have been happy to uncover and upon which time's remedy will depend. The vision of those who build the future Austin will determine whether the new matches the quality of the base. This study is an attempt to help build that vision.

Extracts from A Plan *for the Republic Square District, Austin Texas* for the Watson-Casey Companies, 1984.

Halcyon Ltd., Hartford, CT, Development Consultants. *Project Administrators*: Theodore A. Amenta , Kenn Munkacy, Jerome Rappaport; *With the assistance of*: Michael Buckley, Carl Geupel, Dick Knapp, William Maher and Jim Paresi.
Venturi, Rauch and Scott Brown, Philadelphia, PA, Urban Design. *Principal in Charge*: Denise Scott Brown; *Project Manager*: Vincent Hauser; *Urban Dessign*: Robert Venturi and Miles Ritter; *Project Director*: David Vaughan, Laguna Gloria Art Museum; *With the assistance of*: Margo Angevine, Rick Buckley, Erica Gees, Nancy Goldenberg, Gabrielle London, Bob Marker, John Rauch, Susi Schickendanz, Rob Schwartz, Simon Tickell, James Timberlake and Ann Trowwbridge
Urban Design Consultants:WZMH Group, Inc., Dallas, Tx. Chung Lee, Gregory Powe.
Urban Design and Resource Consultants: Holt+Patter+Scott, Inc., Austin, TX. Joseph J. Holt, Scott Pinkerton, Don Oelfke.
Traffic Consultant: Robert L. Morris Inc., Bathesda, MD.
Resource Consultants: Renfro & Steinbomer Architects, Austin, TX.
Parking Consultants: Merritt A. Neale & Associates, Chevy Chase, MD.
Video Production Facility Consultants: Imero Fiorentino Associates, New York, N.Y. William G. Marshall

OLD VIEW OF AUSTIN

Bibliography

This is a listing of some books and articles that are mentioned in the text, or that are sources for ideas discussed. I have added names of the planning studies described in 'The Rise and Fall of Community Architecture' and also a few items that are relevant to the subjects of this book.

Adams, Gerald D, 'A Last Ditch Effort to Save Downtown San Francisco', *Planning*, February 1984, pp 4–11.

Baldwin, James, 'Letters from a Region in My Mind', *New Yorker*, 17 Nov 1962, pp59–144.

Banham, Reyner, *Theory and Design in the First Machine Age*, New York, Praeger, 1960.

Bauer, Chatherine, *Modern Housing*, Boston/New York, Houghton Mifflin, 1934.

——.'Social Questions in Housing and Community Planning', *of Social Issues*, Vol 7, 1951, p 1.

Brown, Denise Scott, *Report on the Neighbouhood Garden Association*, for the Executive Committee of the Neighborhood Garden Association, Philadelphia, Pa, 1963.

——.'Team 10, Perspecta 10, and the Present State of Architectural Theory', *Journal of the American Institute of Planners*, January 1967, pp 42–50.

——.'Little Magazines in Architecture and Urbanism', *Journal of the American Institute of Planners*, July 1968, pp 223–33.

——.'Urban Structuring', *Architectural Design*, January 1968, p 7 (Review of *Urban Structuring: Studies of Alison and Peter Smithson*).

——.'On Pop Art, Permissiveness and Planning', *Journal of the American Institute of Planners*, May 1969, pp 184–6.

——.'Learning from Pop' and 'Reply to Frampton', *Casabella*, May–June 1971, pp 14–46. Reprinted in *Journal of Popular Culture*, Fall 1973, pp 387–401 and in *View from the Campidoglio*, Robert Venturi and Denise Scott Brown, New York, Harper & Row, 1984, pp 26–34.

——.'An Alternate Proposal that Builds on the Character and Population of South Street', *Architectural Forum*, October 1971, pp 42–44.

——.'On Architectural Formalism and Social Concern: A Discourse for Social Planners and Radical Chic Architects', *Opposition 5*, Summer 1976, pp 99–112.

——.'Revitalising Miami', *Urban Design International*, January–February 1980, pp 20–5.

——.'Architectural Taste in a Pluralistic Society', *The Harvard Architectural Review*, Spring 1980, pp 41–51.

——.'An Urban Design Plan', *Design Quarterly*, Vol 117, 1982, pp 12–23 (on Hennepin Avenue, Minneapolis).

——.'Drawing for the Deco District', *Archithese*, 4 March 1982, pp 17–21.

——.'Visions of the Future Based on Lessons from the Past', *Center*, Vol 1, 1985, pp 44–63; also published in *The Land, The City, and the Human Spirit*, Larry Fuller, ed, University of Texas: LBJ Library, 1985, pp 108–14 and panel discussion, pp 128–36 (plan for the Republic Square District Austin).

——.'From Memphis, Down the Mississippi to the World', Forward to *Memphis: 1948–1958*, Memphis Brooks Museum of Art, 1986, pp viii–xi.

——.'My Miami Beach', *Interview*, September 1986, pp 156–8.

——.'Interview with Denise Scott Brown', by Tom Killian and Francoise Astorg Bollack in *Everyday Masterpieces: Memory and Modernity*, Modena, Italy: Edizioni Panini, 1988, (Deco architecture, Miami Beach).

——.'Learning from Brutalism', essay prepared for *The Independent Group* exhibition catalogue scheduled for February 1990, Institute of Contemporary Art, London, England. New York, Hudson Hills Press, 1990.

Bruchell, Robert W and George Sternlieb, eds, *Planning Theory in the 1980s: A Search for Future Directions*, New Brunswick, N J, Center for Urban Policy Research, Rutgers University, 1979.

Burnham, Daniel H and Edward Bennett, ed. Charles Moore, *Plan for Chicago*, Chicago, Ill, The Commercial Club, 1909, reprinted, New York, Da Capo Press, 1970.

Crane, David A, 'Chandigarh Reconsidered: The Dynamic City', *Journal of the American Insitutute of Architects*, May 1960, pp 32–9.

——.'The City Symbolic', *The Journal of the American Institute of Planners*, November 1960, pp 280–292.

Cranz, Galen, *The Politics of Park Design: A History of Urban Parks in America*, Cambridge, Mass, MIT Press, 1982.

Davidoff, Paul and Thomas Reiner, 'A Choice Theory of Planning', *American Institute of Planners Journal*, May 1962, pp 103–15.

Davidoff, Paul, 'Advocacy and Pluralism in Planning',

Journal of the American Institute of Planners, November 1965, pp 331–8.

——.'The Redistributive Function in Planning: Creating Greater Equity Among Citizens of Communities', *Planning Theory in the 1980s: A Search for Future Directions*, eds. Robert W Burchell and George Sternlieb, New Brunswick, N J, Center for Urban Policy Research, Rutgers University, 1979, pp 69–72.

Dyckman, John W, 'Three Crises of American Planning', *Planning Theory in the 1980s: A Search for Future Directions*, eds. Robert W Burchell and George Sternlieb, New Brunsiwck, N J, Center for Urban Policy Research, Rutgers University, 1979, pp 279–95.

Ferebee, Ann, ed *Education for Urban Design: Proceedings of the Urban Design Educators' Retreat*, Purchase, N Y, Institute for Urban Design, 1982.

Galbraith, John Kenneth, *The Affluent Society*, Boston, Mass, Houghton Mifflin Co, 1958.

Gans, Herbert J, *The Urban Villagers: Group and Class in the Life of Italian–Americans*, Glencoe, Ill, The Free Press, 1962.

——.'City Planning and Urban Realities', *Commentary*, February 1962, pp 170–5.

——.*The Levittowners: Ways of Life and Politics in a New Suburban Community*, New York, Columbia University Press, 1967.

——.*People and Plans: Essays on Urban Problems and Solutions*, New York, Basic Books, 1968.

——.*Popular Cutlure and High Culture: an Analysis and Evaluation of Taste*, New York, Basic Books Inc, 1974.

——.*Middle American Individualism: The Future of Liberal Democracy*, New York, The Free Press, 1988.

Goodman, Paul and Percival, *Communitas: Ways of Livelihood and Means of Life*, New York, Random House Inc, 1947.

Harrington, Michael, *The Other America: Poverty in the United States*, New York, Macmillan, 1964.

——.*The New American Poverty*, New York, Holt, Rinehart & Winston, 1984.

Hatt, Paul K and Albert J Reiss, Jr, eds, *Cities and Society: The Revised Reader in Urban Sociology*, Glencoe, Ill, The Free Press, 1957.

Hitchcock, Henry Russell and Philip Johnson, *The International Style: Architecture since 1922*, New York, W W Norton & Co, 1932, reprint 1966.

Isard, Walter, *Location and Space–Economy: A General Theory Relating to Industrial Location, Market Areas, Land–Use, Trade, and Urban Structure*, Cambridge, Mass, MIT Press, 1956.

Jackson, John Brinckerhoff, *Landscapes: Selected Writings of J B Jackson*, ed. Ervin H Zube, Amherst, University of Massachusetts Press, 1970.

——.*The Interpretation of Ordinary Landscapes: Georgraphical Essays*, ed. D W Meinig, New York, Oxford University Press, 1979.

——.*The Necessity for Ruins and Other Topics*, Amherst, University of Massachusetts, 1980.

——.*Discovering the Vernacular Landscape*, New Haven, Yale University Press, 1984.

Jacobs, Jane, *Death and Life of Great American Cities*, New York, Vintage Books, 1961.

Jenkins, Simon, 'British Renaissance Reborn', *The Sunday Times* (London) 18 April 1987, p 25.

Korn, Arthur, *History Builds the Town*, London, Lund, Humphries, 1953.

Kriesis, Paul, *Three Essays on Town Planning*, St. Louis, Mo, The School of Architecture, Washington University, May 1963.

Le Corbusier, *Towards a New Architecture*, 1923, Trans, Frederick Etchells, 1927, London, The Architectural Press, 1946.

Lilla, Mark, 'The Great Museum Muddle', *The New Republic*, 8 April 1985, pp 25–30.

Lynch, Kevin, 'The Form of Cities', *Scientific American*, April 1954.

Maki, Fumihiko, *Investigations in Collective Form*, St Louis, Mo, The School of Architecture, Washington University, June 1964.

Mitchell, RB and C Rapkin, *Urban Traffic, A Function of Land Use*, New York, Columbia University Press, 1954.

Moore, Charles W, 'You have to Pay for the Public Life', *Perspecta*, No 9/10, 1965, pp 57–106.

Mumford, Lewis, *The Lewis Mumford Reader*, ed. Donald L Miller, New York, Pantheon Books, 1986.

Myerson, Martin & Edward C Banfield, *Politics, Planning and the Public Interest*, The case of Public Housing in Chicago, Glencoe, Ill, Free Press, 1955.

Pawley, Martin, 'P S. Martin Pawley Takes a Look at the Real Heroes of CAD', *Royal Institute of British Architects Journal*, April 1988, p 50.

Seeger, Charles, 'Preface to the Critique of Music', *1st Inter–American Conference on Ethnomusicology: Cartagena de Indieas 1963*, p 39.

——.'The Music Process as a Function in a Context of Function', *Yearbook, Inter–American Institute for Musical Research*, Vol II, 1966, pp 1–36.

——.'Towards a Unitary Field Theory for Musicology', *Selected Reports*, Vol. 1/3, 1970, pp 171–120.

——.'Tractatus Estehico–semioticus', *Current Thoughts in Musicology*, ed, J W, Grubbs and L Perkins, Austin, Texas, 1976.

Smithson, Alison, ed. 'Team 10 Primer', *Architectural Design*, May 1960, pp 175–205, reprinted, *Team 10 Primer*, Cambridge, Mass, The MIT Press, 1968.

Smithson, Alison and Peter Smithson, *Uppercase 3*, Ltd. ed. London, Whitefriar Press, 1960.

Summerson, John, *Georgian London*, 3rd edition, Cambridge Mass, MIT Press, 1978.

Tyrwhitt, Jacqueline, ed. *Patrick Geddes in India*, (Extracts from official reports on Indian cities in 1915–19) London, Lund, Humphries, 1947.

Venturi, Robert, *Complexity and Contradiction in Architecture*, New York, Museum of Modern Art and Graham Foundation, 1966.

——.'RIBA Discourse, July 1981', *Transactions 1*, the Royal Institute of British Architects, May 1982, pp 47–56. Reprinted in *View from the Campidoglio*, Robert Venturi and Denise Scott Brown, New York, Harper & Row, 1984, pp 104–107.

——..'Diversity, Relevance and Representation in Historicism, or Plus ca Change ... plus a Plea for Pattern all over Architecture with a Postscript on my Mother's House', *Architectural Record*, June 1982, pp 114–19. Reprinted in *View from the Campidoglio*, Robert Venturi and Denise Scott Brown, New York, Harper & Row, 1984, pp 108–19.

——.'From Invention to Convention in Architecture', *RSA Journal*, 28 January 1988, pp 89–103.

Venturi, Robert, Denise Scott Brown and Steven Izenour, *Learning from Las Vegas*, Cambridge, Mass, MIT Press, 1972. Revised 1977 (1972 edition contains description of South Street project).

Venturi, Rauch and Scott Brown, *Fairmont Manor and the Poplar Community*, prepared for the U S Department of Housing and Urban Development, H U D, 1973.

——.*Historic Jim Thorpe: a Study of the Old Mauch Chunk Historic District*, prepared for the Carbon County Planning Commission, Jim Thorpe, Pa, 1979, unpublished.

——.*City of Miami Beach, Washington Avenue Revitalisation Plan*, prepared for the Miami Beach Planning Department, Florida, 1979, unpublished.

——.*Princeton Urban Design Study*, prepared for the Borough of Princeton, New Jersey, 1980, unpublished.

——.*The Hennepin Avenue Study*, prepared for Minneoplis Planning Department Minneapolis, Mn, 1981.

——.*A Plan for the Republic Square District*, prepared for the Watson–Casey Companies, Austin, Texas, 1984.

——.*Center City Development Plan for Downtown Memphis*, prepared for the Center City Commission, Memphis, Tennessee, 1987, unpublished.

Wagner, Philip L, *The Human Use of the Earth*, Glencoe, Ill, The Free Press, 1960.

Webber, Melvin, M, 'Comprehensive Planning and Social Responsibility', *American Institute of Planners Journal*, Vol. 29, No 4, 1963, pp 232–41.

——.'The New Urban Planning in America', *Town Planning Institute Journal*, Vol. 54,January 1968, pp 3–10.

——.'Planning in an Environment of Change', *Town Planning Review*, Vol. 39, No 3, October 1968, pp 179–95; Vol. 39, No 4, January 1969, pp 277–95.

——.'The Role of Intelligence Systems in Urban–systems Planning', *American Institute of Planners Journal*, Vol. 31, No 4, November 1965, pp 289–96.

——.'A Difference Paradigm for Planning', *Planning Theory in the 1980s: A Search for Future Directions*, ed. Robert W Burchell and George Sternlieb, New Brunswick, N J, Center for Urban Policy Research, 1979.

Whyte, William H, *The Social Life of Small Urban Spaces*, Washington D C, The Conservation Foundation, 1980.

Williams, George A, 'Fine Points of the San Francisco Plan', *Planning*, February 1984, pp 12–15.

Young, Michael and Peter Willmott, *Family and Kinship in East London*, London, Routledge & Kegan Paul, 1957.